DR. SAMUEL MAINOO

THE MARRIAGE FOR SERIOUS MINDS

Love-Need Vow Responsibilities of Marriage

The Marriage for Serious Minds

Copyright ©2021 Samuel Mainoo

ISBN: 978-1-7373966-0-4

Published by Eyes of Heart Publishers, LLC
3590 Morinda Drive
Douglasville, GA 30135

All rights reserved, comprising the rights to reproduce this publication in any form or kind, such as electronic, mechanical, photocopying, recording, and in any way possible without the prior permission of the publisher, except as provided by USA copyright law.

Eyes of Heart Publishers is a registered trademark in the United States of America.

Cover Design and Typesetting: Niivive LLC, USA

First printing: 2021
Printed in the United States of America

All scripture quotations are from The Holy Bible: New King James Version (NKJV), unless otherwise indicated. New King James Version; Copyright © 1982 by Thomas Nelson. Used by permission. All rights reserved.

For marriage, family and singles' seminar or conference; or for spouses' and individual counseling; or for revival speaking engagements, kindly reach us at the following contacts: raphacounselingsolutions@gmail.com or sm@raphacounselingsolutions.com

Printed in the United States of America

TABLE OF CONTENTS

Dedication	*v*
Acknowledgments	*vi*
Synopsis of The Book	*viii*
Introduction	*x*

PART 1 - Building the Success Foundation of Your Marriage — 14
Chapter 1 : The Destroyed Foundation of Marriage — 15
Chapter 2 : Building the Four Success Marriage Pillars — 21
Chapter 3 : The Five Marital Love-Need Vow Witnesses — 37
Chapter 4 : The Aloneness and Loneliness Problems and Solutions — 45
Chapter 5 : Marital Agreement Needs Principles. — 53

PART 2 - Comprehensive Biblical Definition of Marriage with Its Seventeen Principles — 60
Chapter 1 : Comprehensive Biblical Meaning of Marriage — 61
Chapter 2 : Seventeen Principles of The Meaning of Marriage — 63

PART 3 - Love Definition with Its Three Dimensions. — 90
Chapter 1 : Meaning of Love — 91
Chapter 2 : General Expectational Love (GEL) — 95
Chapter 3 : The Multifunctional Applied Love (MAL) — 97
Chapter 4 : The Exclusive Reciprocal Obligatory Love (EROL) — 99

PART 4 - The Four Exclusive Reciprocal Obligatory Love (EROL) — 102
Chapter 1 : The Exclusive Reciprocal Obligatory Wife's Love of Affection — 103
Chapter 2 : The Exclusive Reciprocal Obligatory Husband's Love of Respect — 109
Chapter 3 : The Exclusive Reciprocal Obligatory Love of Romance — 119
Chapter 4 : The Exclusive Reciprocal Obligatory Love of Intimacy — 125

PART 5 - The Love-Need Vow Purpose of Marriage   132

Chapter 1 : Indispensable Love-Need Purpose of Marriage   133
Chapter 2 : Meaning of Vow with Its Implications in Marriage   137

PART 6 - The Ten Love-Need-Vow Responsibilities of Marriage   140

Chapter 1 : Vow to Leave Behind All Intrusions Against Your Marriage for Lifetime   141
Chapter 2 : Vow to Love Each Other With the Seven Multifunctional Applied Love (MAL) for Lifetime   161
Chapter 3 : Vow to Fulfil the Five Needs of Companionship for Lifetime   189
Chapter 4 : Vow to Keep the Marriage Bed Pure for Lifetime.   207
Chapter 5 : Vow to Express the Eight Honoring Virtues to Your Spouse for Lifetime   215
Chapter 6 : Vow to Serve Your Spouse for Lifetime   233
Chapter 7 : Vow to Make Each Other Happy for Lifetime   239
Chapter 8 : Vow to Readily Admit and Forgive Faults for Lifetime   243
Chapter 9 : Vow to Have All Things in Common for Lifetime   257
Chapter 10 : Vow to Choose the Right Marital Financial Plan for Lifetime   267

DEDICATION

To my lovely wife and children

ACKNOWLEDGMENTS

First and foremost, my indescribable heartfelt gratitude goes to the Almighty God for granting me the insights of wisdom, understanding, and the strength to complete the all-in-one efficient principles for marital success and happiness book: The Marriage for Serious Minds: The Need-Vow Duties of Marriage.

Second, a great appreciation goes to my wonderful wife, and our lovely children for their love, great support, motivation, patience, and prayers which have helped me to get this great work done. Thus, to my lovely and wonderful wife, Helga, much love to you; and to our blessed children: Samuel Jr., Lemuel, Excellin, Uriel, Alexia, Aristarcus and Jedidah, much love to every one of you. I also want to acknowledge my late, Diana for her great support for me in the early part and course of my life and ministry. May your soul continue to rest in the very perfect peace of our Lord and Savior Jesus Christ.

Third, a special appreciation goes to my mother, Mary, for all her indescribable love investments in my life. Fourth to my parent in-laws for their moral support. Fifth appreciation goes to all the Ghanaian Ministers Association of Georgia for their moral support and prayers.

Sixth, a heartfelt gratitude goes to a dear friend and a brother in ministry, Rev. Dr. Robert Yaw Owusu who helped with the proofreading and writing synopsis for this book. Seventh appreciation goes to Apostle Joseph Agyapong (General Overseer of GCGM), all the pastors and members of Global Church of Grace Ministries USA for their prayer support.

The last but not the least appreciation goes to my late spiritual father and coach and his late wife, Bishop Stephen, and Lady Evelyn Tchie for helping me build the right foundation for my call and ministry. Not forgetting all the pastors and members of Pentecostal Life Church International, Ghana of which I was a pastor for over eleven years.

SYNOPSIS OF THE BOOK

In this book the author, Dr. Samuel Mainoo, will stimulate you to read on to the end. There is logical flow of the contents which means the book is well-structured like a house built from the ground (foundation) to the roof top. Do not start reading from the last chapter but from the first to the last and you will reap the benefits of the time and efforts spent.

Today, it is quite a challenge to talk or write on marriage centered on biblical principles, yet Rev. Dr. Mainoo embarks on this journey to remind us of the root of marriage between a man and a woman, especially the implications of the vows, spouses take. Consequently, the principles advocated in this book are built on biblical thoughts and foundation. "By principle," says the author, "if spouses make the effort to discover and apply the truths about marital happiness and success, it will guarantee their freedom from deception, confusion, and struggle. The freedom that comes by knowing and applying the marital truth leads to the know-how confidence of handling marital challenges with ease." (p. 17)

The book has what I call built-in terminologies, concepts, idioms, and metaphors to which one needs to pay attention. Fortunately, the author has taken his time to define and clarify these concepts or linguistic complex.

According to the author, "Right knowledge about anything leads to the appropriate application with its subsequent success" (p. 17). This is insightful not only to marital relations but to all our human endeavors. I heartily recommend this book to you and would urge you to read to the end.

By Dr. Robert Yaw Owusu

INTRODUCTION

THE MARRIAGE FOR SERIOUS MINDS

The The Marriage for Serious Minds is about the love-need vow duties of marriage, detailing an all-in-one efficient counseling principles for marital success and happiness. Marriage requires spouses to ceaselessly meet their indispensable or crying needs, being motivated by their own love-vows. The Marriage for Serious Minds is indeed for the serious minds as it is titled. In fact, the marriage charge in all the Ministers Manuals I have used for officiating marriages, advise against entering marriage without the seriousness it requires. [1]Nelson's Ministers Manual puts it this way: "…marriage is commended in the scriptures to be honorable among all, and therefore is not by any to be entered into unadvisedly or lightly, but reverently, discreetly, advisedly, soberly, and in in the fear of God (p.15) …"

The reason for this biblical recommendation is that marriage requires the full assumption of its love-need vow duties in order for it to produce the happiness and success results. When spouses knowingly or unknowingly and con-

---
1. Nelson, Thomas, *Nelson's Minister's Manual* (Nashville: Thomas Nelson, 2003), 15.

sciously or unconsciously fail to fulfill these crying or indispensable love-need vow duties to each other, the happiness and the security of their marriage becomes compromised. Hence, struggles and probable irresolvable conflicts. It is said that "no well-sounded person marries their own enemy (source unknown)." However, in so many marriages worldwide, it turns out that the very loveliest and dearest person one could not wake up without dreaming about, later turns up to become a bitterest enemy. In such situations to some extent, the spouses find it difficult to see eye to eye in the course of time.

The good thing, however, is this, when the needs of each spouse are continuously met, it generates higher attractiveness, endearment, vitality, happiness, and satisfaction. On the other hand, when these indispensable needs are denied and neglected for a longer time, it reduces the endearment of each other into nothingness of confusion, frustration, anger, and subsequent decline of the marriage. If your marriage has either become boring, fallen sick and suffering or doing well, this book is for you.

The Marriage for Serious Minds as already emphasized is an all-in-one efficient step by step marital principles for successful marriages and happy spouses. The book is designed to accomplish three goals in marriage: Guide to constructing or reconstructing the right and solid marital foundation, erecting the right pillars to hold the marriage, and building the magnificent structure of beauty, happiness, and success every spouse desire in their marriage.

In building your marriage on these well-founded foundational principles in this book, your marriage shall turn around, start growing, glowing, and bearing abundant fruit of happiness and success you never thought possible or ever dreamed about. It is indeed true that *"you shall know the truth and the truth shall make you free (John 8:32)."* In other words, when you make the necessary effort to discover the needed truth for your life or in any area of your life, you will no longer be in bondage to any manipulative lies of the devil about this life with all its endeavors.

The Marriage for Serious Minds is divided into six parts, and each part is loaded with chapters providing principles and guides to enriching marriages and empowering spouses to enjoy the best of their marriage. In summary, part one deals with Building the Success Foundation of Your Marriage. Part two is about the Comprehensive Biblical Meaning of Marriage with Its Seventeen Principles. Part three deals with Love Meaning with its Three Dimensions. Part four is about the Four Exclusive Reciprocal Obligatory Love (EROL). Part five, the Love-Need Vow Purpose of Marriage. Lastly, the part six deals with the Ten Love-Need Vow Duties of Marriage.

All the principles in this book are outlined and explained in detail and its six sections provide the keys to unlocking the happiness, success, and the security you have been wondering and seeking for in all your marital life. I, therefore, encourage all my readers to develop their willingness to discover the truth and principles which require serious minds to embrace and apply, because it will ensure the blissful expectation of every spouse and yet to be spouses.

Once again, I would like to encourage you to read and read on to the very end of this book to ascertain its truths and recommendations in toto. By exhausting the content of this book, you are indeed abreasting yourself with the marital answers you have been longing for and searching out to solve your marital confusion and conflict puzzles. I also like to recommend for spouses to keep a copy each and read it once or twice a year and reference it from time to time. May God bless you in this journey of discovery and your pursuit of marital happiness.

PART 1

BUILDING THE SUCCESS FOUNDATION OF YOUR MARRIAGE

Psalm 11:3
*If the foundations are destroyed,
what can the righteous do?*

CHAPTER ONE

THE DESTROYED FOUNDATION OF MARRIAGE

The question is, what is "the destroyed foundation?" The destroyed foundation from biblical perspective and principle is any specific life foundation which has been poorly built to hold its intended structure. Or the "destroyed foundation" is a foundation which has been improperly built and therefore, has been set to fall during the storms of life. Therefore, when foundations are poorly built, pressure from within and without shall result to its fall, causing dangerous damages.

The other question from this passage is, "what can the righteous do?" The answer shall be nothing! The righteous can do nothing, because the righteous has set his or her own future in that particular aspect of life to fail by default. Hence, it does not matter who you are as a child of God, if have built your own foundation to destroy your own future, you have indeed limited God from helping and blessing you succeed.

Unfortunately, God cannot and will not be able to help anybody to build upon destroyed foundations because it goes against His principle of rightness. Another reason is that in all life endeavors, in relation to God, there is always a shared responsibility. There is the human responsibility and God's responsibility in all aspects of human endeavors. So, if a child of God refuses to do his or her part of the success responsibility, God has been limited to do His part. Again, it does not matter whether a person has faith in God or not, building the right foundation for one's own life and marriage is a human responsibility and not a divine one.

Sadly, if you build a destroyed foundation for your marriage, there is nothing God can do about it, despite the unending fasting and prayers. God always would like to invest His divine resources of blessings on the properly built foundations and structures in the lives of humanity. Christ Jesus' three and half years of ministry on earth was concentrated on building a solid foundation in His disciples by equipping and preparing them for efficient and successful missions after his departure. The proper understanding of reconciling humanity back to God and equipping them for the work of the ministry was the foundation Jesus spent the three and half years building in them **(Ephesians 4:11-16)**.

Therefore, if you have poorly built your foundation for your own life and marriage, you have indeed limited God from blessing your life and marriage. In this case, God will not be able to secure and ensure the standing of your marital foundation and what is built upon it. Hence, one has subjected and prepared life and marriage for failure.

Benjamin Franklin, one of the founding fathers of United States of America once said, "if you fail to plan, you are planning to fail" (source unknown). In other words, if you fail to plan or build the right foundation from the very beginning of your future success, you have indeed planned your future to fail. In such circumstances, one may tend to blame it on others, but the fact is that it is oneself that is to be blamed.

Every successful venture in this life requires some solid form of foundation of right knowledge and understanding. Marriage as an honorable and beautiful union requires its foundation to be built right from its very beginning. The reason is that building the right foundation for your marriage directly affects everything in your life and the marriage itself. As indelibly important marriage is, it requires a well-grounded foundation and understanding to make it thrive and succeed with great happiness and satisfaction. Failure to build a solid foundation for your marriage is to set your marriage up for failure sooner or later.

In building solid foundation for the success and happiness of your marriage, you must develop the mindset to understand and apply the principles of constructing the foundation of your marriage aright from its very beginning. However, if you are already married and have built a destroyed foundation for your marriage, it is not too late to renovate and reinforce it with the right knowledge and understanding for its success as outlined and explained in the following parts and chapters.

Furthermore, Dr. Arthur F. Holmes, who was a professor at Wheaton College affirms a deep truth in his book, entitled, [2]"All Truth is God's Truth." This means that all truth has their source from God, no matter who discovered it and where it originated from. Truth is universal and must be applicable to all people. Therefore, a particular truth may be from the Bible, religion, philosophy, or science, it is still God's truth, and it could be applicable to [3]"all people, at all places and at all times (Dr. Frank Turek, from one of his lectures on Cross Examined)."

If a particular truth cannot be applied to all people, at all places, and at all times, as indicated above, then such truth must be questioned because it does not meet the standards or the requirements of truth. My point here is that building the right and good lasting foundation for any structure is a universal truth and it is applicable to all people, at all places, and at all times. Hence, the truth principles of this book are from a biblical perspective, and it is applicable to all marriages of all people, at all times, and at all places. In order words, no matter the culture, the principles in this book are sure to work for your marital success and happiness.

Again, regarding proper and improper foundation building, Jesus underscores it with a profound scenario as stated in **Matthew 7:24-27** *"Therefore whoever hears these sayings of Mine, and does them, I will liken him to* **a wise man who built his house on the rock:** [25]*"and the rain de-*

---
2. Arthur F. Holmes, *All Truth is God's Truth* (Downers Grove: Inter-Varsity press, 1979).
3. (Dr. Frank Turek, from Q & A on Cross Examine, https://crossexamined.org/)."

*scended, the floods came, and the winds blew and beat on that house; and **it did not fall, for it was founded on the rock**.* *²⁶"But everyone who hears these sayings of Mine, and does not do them, **will be like a foolish man who built his house on the sand**: ²⁷"and the rain descended, the floods came, and the winds blew and beat on that house; and it fell. **And great was its fall.**"*

The purpose of this book, therefore, is focused on guiding married and yet-to-be-married couples to build the right and solid foundation for their marriage. It shall also provide the systematic guide to building on the foundation for the desired success and happiness every spouse expects in their marriages.

Therefore, my appeal to all readers of this book is for them to read to the end and apply its principles in the best way possible, and you shall never regret you did. This is because every marital precept in this book is built upon its foundational precept to ultimately chart out the way to happiness and the success spouses expect in their marriages. One of the first things to embark on to enable spouses to chart out this success path is the readiness to build the four success marriage pillars.

CHAPTER TWO

BUILDING THE FOUR SUCCESS MARRIAGE PILLARS

If you are willing and obedient, you shall eat the good of the land
(Isaiah 1:19)

The four success pillars in marriage are the four cornerstones which hold the marital structure of success and happiness together. These pillars are goal directed to enhance the understanding of what is expected of anyone who decides to marry or is already in marriage. It is always expedient to abide by the principles and vow duties of marriage in order to experience its success and happiness.

The scriptural verse above affirms that willingness and obedience pave way to happiness and success as stated *"… you shall eat the good of the land"*. Embedded within the two pillars of willingness and obedience mentioned in the text above are knowledge and love. Hence, the four foundational success pillars to be applied to marriage are: Willingness, knowledge, love, and obedience.

1. BUILDING YOUR MARITAL PILLAR OF WILLINGNESS

The first pillar of marital success and happiness is willingness as stated in the text above, *"if you are willing…"* Before a couple comes to the voluntary agreement to marry, each one must ask himself or herself respectively and ask the same follow up questions of each other: Are you willing to adjust to the new life of marriage with its love-need vow duties? And are you willing to faithfully assume and adhere to the marital love-need vow duties? The importance of asking these willingness questions cannot be over emphasized. The reason being that such willingness is what is going to determine the seriousness to building the marital foundation and its pillars alright with its beautiful structure to be enjoyed from year to year.

The mental, emotional, and volitional (will) preparation toward marriage is the foundation to assure each other of marital working efficiency. Marital efficiency is the willingness from each spouse to do the right things of marriage right, at the right time with the right motive and commitment, being motivated by love, admiration, respect, and endearment. The marital pillar of willingness cannot be built alone, rather it supposed to be built together with its seven supportive pillars. Therefore, building the marital pillar of willingness shall require every spouse's commitment to building these additional seven willing supportive pillars as follows:

1. **Willingness to Surrender Selfishness and Self-centeredness** – In building the pillar of willingness, the spouses must commit to surrender or let go of selfishness and self-centeredness in order to meet the love-needs of each other. Spouses must be willing to sacrifice selfishness and self-centeredness which usually wield the propensity to stop each spouse from pleasing and meeting each other's love-needs. The willingness and the commitment to please each other is the pathway to marital happiness.

    In fact, after marriage, life is no more about self, but it is about each other. Every spouse must always remember that the ultimate requirement of marriage is to willingly commit to fulfill the love-needs your spouse cannot live to enjoy the marriage without. If your spouse is compelling you to meet his or her love-needs, you have failed as a spouse. The unloving behavior like this in marriage does not only affect one spouse, but it rather affects both spouses' happiness and the success of the marriage.

    The reason is that the better the emotional health of your spouse, the better your own emotional health. The fact of the matter is that as spouses starve each other emotionally by refusing to meet each other's love-needs, the emotional health of each other becomes compromised. This is because such behavior in marriage arouses unhealthy or toxic emotions which shall intend begin to impede the health and the happiness of each spouse.

2. **Willingness to Adjust** - In building the pillar of willingness, the spouses must commit to adjust and adapt. The spouses' willingness to adjust and adapt to the new life of the marriage require them to invest their time, attention, energy, and patience on each other intentionally. The willingness to adjust must be motivated by love to bring about compatibility or agreement in the marital relationship. The willingness to adjust yourself to your spouse makes each other suitable to each other in the marriage.

When God instituted marriage, He gave Eve to Adam and required her to go and provide the suitable help Adam shall need to enjoy her and succeed in the marriage. He also required Adam to receive her as his bone of his bones and flesh of his own flesh in order to enjoy her and succeed in the marriage **(Genesis 2:20; 23).**

Being suitable or comparable to each other in marriage requires adjustment from the single life into the oneness of the new joint life of marriage. Before and after the marriage, the single old self of selfishness and self-centeredness must willingly give way to the new joint life of the marriage. The old single life must transition into the new joint-life which is adjusted by selflessness and sacrifice of love into oneness of marital success and happiness. There are many who have married and yet have refused to transition from old self of the single life into the new joint-life of the marriage. The unwillingness to transition after marriage is sure to generate unnecessary tensions and conflicts.

3. **Willingness to Bring About Resolution** – The building of the willingness pillar requires the spouses to build the supportive pillar of resolution. The love-need of spouses require them to develop the willingness to resolve any marital conflict they may encounter in the course of the marriage. The spouses are therefore required to develop the mindset to accept marital problems as challenges and not as burdens. Relational conflicts should not be only considered as negative but also as positive. The reason being that conflicts by nature supposed to show the spouses where attention and loving talk of resolution are needed.

Spouses must understand that their differences in upbringing, temperaments, exposure, perception, and various familiarities of life, can easily arouse conflict of disagreements. However, the spouses must remember that marital conflict's unrealized secret benefit is the awareness of each other's strengths and weaknesses, which require attention to bring about resolution of agreement. The conflict of disagreement in marriage is inevitable and all what it requires is the attention of adjustment to bring about agreement.

Marital adjustment to bring about resolution is not a one-time effort and must not become a nine-day wonder. Rather, it must be a conscious and committed exercises for lifetime in order for the spouses to enjoy their marriage. The willingness to adjust to please each other, the better the enjoyment of the marriage. The strength of each other should always inspire appreciation and encouragement. The knowledge of each other's weaknesses should inspire patience of tolerance and better communication of resolution in order to encourage change for a better life in the marriage.

4. **Willingness to Exercise All-In-Common Principles** - Spouses must be willing to have all things in common selflessly and cheerfully, for the mutual benefit, and enjoyment. Marriage requires partnership and oneness of everything for the betterment of each spouse. If a person is not willing to avail everything and to lay bare everything to the marriage, true cleaving or bonding of hearts and body cannot be realized in the marriage.

The number one cause of marital conflict is the ego of selfishness, self-centeredness, greed, and pride. To marry and still live in your own self-motivated world is a separation of self from the active relationship and duties of the marriage, leading to a day-to-day decline of the life and health of the marriage. The particularly important thing many spouses forget about is that marriage is not about self, but it is about one's own spouse's happiness and wellbeing. The commitment to fulfill the love-need of your spouse, is the assurance of fulfilling your own love-needs.

However, if a spouse marries and focus on what he or she can benefit from the other spouse, the marriage has been preset to arouse confusion, conflicts and decline of the marital relationship. In other words, if a person decides to marry to please self, such a person is not ready for marriage. However, when such a self-centered person marries, troubles and confusion shall be the unfortunate state of the marital relationship. The troubled state of the marriage shall then arouse negative emotions of hurts, frustration, and bitterness, which are sure to poison the health of the marital relationship.

5. **Willingness to Trust** - The building of the willingness pillar requires the spouses to build the supportive pillar of trust. Spouses must be willing to trust and lay vulnerable to each other by the motivation of love. Spouses who are bonded in true love shall never do anything to cause any emotional harm or damage to each person intentionally as affirmed in Romans 13:10; *Love does no harm to a neighbor; therefore, love is the fulfillment of the law* (**Romans 13:10**).

In the same way, true loving spouses should not give room for their spouses to fear and be suspicious of them. Neither should a loving spouse think and plan evil against each other as also affirmed in **John 4:18;** *"There is no fear in love; but perfect love casts out fear, because fear involves torment. But he who fears has not been made perfect in love."*

Marital decision should therefore, rest on the fact of trust and vulnerability. If a person sees red flags of distrust and still commit to become vulnerable by love to marry, that person have indeed opened up self for foreseeable heartbreaks. Whoever decides to marry, should endeavor to marry a person who can be trusted in order to secure a peaceful mind and promising future.

Love of trust relieves a spouse from the fear of evil intentions, infidelities, rejection, and abandonment. Lack of trust develops the entertaining of fears, and such timidity causes love to fall short of genuineness. Distrustful perceptions cause undue emotional and mental torment which usually rob its victims of their happiness in the marriage. For this reason, it is advisable to marry a person you can trust and love vulnerably with the assurance and knowledge that he or she shall never betray your trust of vulnerability. But shall rather be sincerely looking out for your wellbeing fir lifetime.

6. **Willingness to Admit Fault** - The building of the willingness pillar requires the spouses to build the supportive pillar of fault admittance. Spouses must be willing to admit faults and must be accountable to each other with the acknowledgement of one's own weaknesses. The reason being that "to err is human." When faults are brought to each other's attention, each spouse must be willing to exercise the courtesy to accept it without arguing or disputing. The offending spouse should rather apologize quickly to acknowledge imperfections or humanness and make the necessary and genuine amends it requires.

Again, spouses must realize that they are accountable to each other. Marital accountability assigns to each spouse the responsibility to make known everything about themselves to each other. Accountability in marriage grants each spouses the right of full knowledge of each other and thought life. Marital accountability is required of each spouse to have the willingness to share everything that goes on in each other's life and mind. To encourage familiarity and closeness, conversation of each day's activities and experiences should be shared and be received with focused attention. Accountability in marital relationship also requires each other to take up the responsibility as the keeper and protector of each other.

7. **Willingness to Maximize Strengths** - The building of the willingness pillar requires the spouses to build the supportive pillar of maximizing strengths of each other as spouses. Spouses must, therefore, develop the willing to maximize each other's character strengths by living them out to please each other by way of minimizing weaknesses.

By principle, weaknesses are usually marginalized and overcome by developing and living out one's own strengths with the goal of pleasing one's own spouse by the motivation of love. Spouses must endeavor to serve each other with their strengths and do well to emphasize and appreciate the strengths of each other. By doing so, each spouse will be motivated to work on their own weaknesses to ensure peace, happiness, and the best of love. The building of the pillar of willingness should lead to the building of the pillar of knowledge.

2. BUILDING YOUR MARITAL PILLAR OF KNOWLEDGE

The building of the marital pillar of knowledge supposed to lead to asking of marital questions of what, why, how, whom, who and when of marriage you do not know. Spouses must search for what they do not know by asking the right questions to unveil the knowledge needed to understand each other. Discovery of the right knowledge and understanding about marriage saves spouses from living out their marital life in assumptions and false perceptions.

Right knowledge about anything leads to the appropriate application with its subsequent success.

Acquiring the right knowledge about marriage shall save the spouses from confusion, irresolvable conflicts and emotional plaguing bitterness which destroys homes and marriages. **John 8:32** affirms this principle as follows, *"And you shall know the truth, and the truth shall make you free."* By principle, if spouses make the effort to discover and apply the truths about marital happiness and success, it will guarantee their freedom from deception, confusion, and struggle. The freedom that comes by knowing and applying the marital truth leads to the know-how confidence of handling marital challenges with ease. The right knowledge about anything leads to the appropriate application with its subsequent success. Hence, developing and applying the right knowledge to your marriage is the key to your marital happiness and success.

Furthermore, spouses must develop the willingness and the desire to seek the right knowledge and understanding of marriage. The spouses can acquire the right knowledge by reading good books about marriage like the one you are reading now and to seek good marriage counseling like the one offered by Rapha Counseling Solutions. The Scriptures recommend to anyone who is seeking for answers to take the following steps: *"Ask, and it will be given to you; seek, and you will find; knock, and it will be opened to you. ⁸"For everyone who asks receives, and he who seeks finds, and to him who knocks it will be opened* **(Matthew 7:7-8).** Below are few examples of marital knowledge every spouse should seek and understand in order to ensure marital happiness and success:

1. The knowledge about the right meaning and perspective of marriage as was instituted by God.
2. The right knowledge and understanding of love for marital happiness and success.
3. The knowledge and understanding of the essence and the love-need based vow responsibilities of marriage.
4. Knowledge and understanding about marital adjustments which undergird the agreement of compatibility among spouses.
5. True knowledge and understanding about sex with its physical, mental, and emotional bonding elements and benefits.
6. Knowledge and understanding about marital financial plans and the willingness to choose the right plan to ensure marital success.

3. BUILDING YOUR MARITAL PILLAR OF LOVE

The importance of building the love pillar for your marriage cannot be overemphasized because love serves as a foundation and a pillar in marriage. The unfortunate misunderstanding about love is that many operate in love with their emotions alone, which is motivated by conditions or circumstances. It must, however, be realized that emotional love which is based on feelings is dependent on either favorable or unfavorable conditions or circumstances. The state of a person's emotions at a particular time always determines either their positive or negative reactions with regards to love.

Overall, true love must not be limited to emotions or feelings but must rather, it must be founded on the following foundation: First, love must be based on the intellect of knowledge, truth and understanding. Second, love must be based on the foundation of the volition of commitment, right decision, and determination to ensure marital happiness and success. Third, love can then be motivated by the emotions of feelings.

If spouses fail to grasp the in toto understanding of love, it shall be difficult to apply love principles. In such situations, the marriage shall tend to run only on the fuel of emotional love which usually runs out of love fuel quickly to stall the vehicle of the marriage in the nowhere of marital world. When this unfortunate situation happens, the marriage shall be left in the middle of the road of confusion, frustration, and anger. However, willingness must lead to knowledge and knowledge must abreast spouses with the right understanding and perspectives of love as listed below and also treated in detail in part three:

1. Love of Commitment - It requires spouses' commitment to adjust, communicate openly and freely, and cleave into oneness of life.
2. Love of Sacrifice – It defaces and undermines selfishness and self-centeredness to the promotion of selflessness and care for each other.

3. Love of Affection – It is the crying love-need of wives.
4. Love of Respect – It is the crying love-need of husbands.
5. Love of Romance – It maintains love of attraction, fun and happiness in the marriage.
6. Love of Intimacy – It is the nakedness love principle of transparency, honesty, trust and one-fleshness of sex.
7. Love of Patience – It involves the commitment to tolerance, endurance, humility, listening, and adjusting of selves to give way to marital compatibility of agreement.

4. BUILDING YOUR MARITAL PILLAR OF OBEDIENCE

"If you are willing and obedient... (Isaiah 1;19)"

Building the pillar of obedience in your marriage is a necessity but not an option to marital success and happiness. Obedience in marriage operates on the principle of mutual submission as affirmed in Ephesians, *submitting to one another in the fear of God (5:21)*. Now that the pillar of willingness, knowledge, and love, have been fully erected, the pillar of obedience should be built to ensure balance for the good standing of the marriage as follows:

1. By the virtue of obedience, spouses must be willing to submit to each other by way of mutual respect and honoring.
2. Spouses must obey each other by lovingly fulfilling their crying love-need vows.
3. Spouses must obey each other by mutual submission to acknowledge themselves as each other's personal advisor. Therefore, spouses must be humble and ready to listen to each other's corrections, suggestions, ideas, and concerns willingly and lovingly.

CHAPTER THREE

THE FIVE MARITAL LOVE-NEED VOW WITNESSES

---

*Yet you say, "For what reason?" Because the LORD has been **witness** between you **and the wife of your youth**, with whom you have **dealt treacherously**; Yet she is your companion and your **wife by covenant*** **(Malachi 2:14).**

God instituted marriage to also attract witnesses, of whom He intended to remind every couple about their lifetime love-need vow commitments to each other. The union of marriage by principle, places the man and the woman under the voluntary vow obligation to fulfill each other's love-needs for lifetime. The witnesses who come to support the couple during the marriage, are intended by God to remind the spouses of their love-need vow responsibilities to each other.

Despite the great increase in the world population and modernizations, many cultures around the world are still encouraging the marital love-need vow reminders by their witnessing presence and supports. The various cultures offer these marital love-need vow reminder witnessing presence and support unknowingly.

It is interesting to know that God was the very first witness of the very first marriage between Adam and his wife. Even as at today, He is still the first witness and shall continue to remain as the first witness of marriages. No matter the cultural variances, God is still the first witness of marriages as the following states: ... *Because the* **LORD** *has been* **witness** *between you and the wife of your youth... (Mal. 2:14).* The following are the five love-need vow reminding witnesses every marital couple should know and understand:

1. DIVINE WITNESS OF THE MARITAL LOVE-NEED VOW REMINDER

God is the originator, the institutor of marriage and the giver of its success and happiness principles. God is also the first love-need vow witness reminder of the first marriage in the garden of Eden. In the first marriage between Adam and Eve, God was the only witness of reminder beside the spouses themselves **(Genesis 2:18-25).** God as the first witness to the marriage of Adam and Eve reminded them of their vow to fulfill their needs of companionship and friendship.

In the scripture above, God was cautioning and at the same time entreating spouses not to deal with each other treacherously or become unfaithful with regards to the vows made to each other during marriage as stated: *Yet you say, "For what reason?" Because the* **LORD has been witness** *between* **you** *and the* **wife** *of your youth, with whom you have dealt* **treacherously**; *Yet she is your* **companion** *and your* **wife by covenant** (**Malachi 2:14**). The stated Scripture above outlines four major principles that spouses need to know as follows:

1. ***...the LORD has been witness between you and the wife of your youth...*:** This statement indicates that God is the witness between a couple who by the motivation of their love gets married. Moreover, God is the one who created the first man and the first woman and instituted the first marriage between them. God as the institutor and the first witness of marriage should remind every spouse about their own love-need vow responsibilities in order not to neglect them and disappointment each other.
2. ***...with whom you have dealt treacherously...*:** Again, this phrase brings out the awareness and caution to the spouses who have made a love pledge to meet each other's emotional and physical needs in order not to deal with each other treacherously or unfaithfully. Thus, they are cautioned not to violate their own love-need pledge in order to cause hurts and displeasures to each other emotionally, mentally, and physically.

3. **...*Yet she is your companion*...:** This phrase also serves as a reminder to spouses not to forget their companionship responsibilities to each other. Companionship responsibilities in marriage comprises and requires partnership, confidant-friendship, attention, complementarity, and togetherness. God as the institutor and the very first witness of heterosexual marriage should always remind and challenge all spouses of every culture of their love-need vow responsibilities in order to meet each other's practical companionship needs as listed above. The five companionship marital love-need requirements and principles listed above are fully expatiated upon in part six of chapter three.

4. **...*and your wife by covenant*...:** Furthermore, this phrase indicates that marriage is built on covenant or vow pledge which requires each spouse's commitment to fulfill them to each other. One fact of marriage is that the spouses cannot force or compel each other to love each other because love by nature is freely given and freely received. Individual can compel self to love another but if an individual is forced to express love, its outcome should be considered fake.

   Spouses must always remind themselves that they are in each other's life because they have made a lasting love covenant to meet each other's love needs for lifetime. Love covenant in marriage is voluntary but yet a binding agreement. Therefore, if you are not ready to commit to a love covenant of commitment, please, do not marry because by default you have set the pace to hurt yourself and your covenant partner. Marriage should never be treated with trial and luck mindset. Rather, it should be respected, taken seriously and its principles adhered to voluntarily and lovingly for the success of the marriage and the happiness of each other.

2. FAMILY WITNESS OF THE MARITAL LOVE-NEED VOW REMINDER

Spouses should always remember that the family members who stood with them during their marriage are all witness reminder of their marital love-need vow responsibilities to each other. The very desires and hopes of all family member witnesses are to see the newlywed's enjoyment of happiness and success of their marriage. The family witnesses must always remind the spouses that they have made a vow to fulfill or meet each other's love-needs for their lifetime.

Spouses must therefore, pledge to themselves not to become unfaithful to their own love-vows to meet each other's needs. Remaining faithful to your own love-vows to meet your spouse's needs is by principle, meeting your own needs. The rational is that one can only reap what has been sown. For this reason, spouses must sow the seed of love in their spouse in order to ensure their own enjoyment of love and happiness.

3. CIVIL WITNESS OF MARITAL LOVE-NEED VOW REMINDER

The court system also serves as a witness to the love-need vows of the marriage. In some cases, the court will require couples to seek counseling and submit a report before the marriage can be initiated or endorsed by the authorities of state or the nation. The purpose of this required counseling is to help the spouses understand how marriage works and how they must commit to meet each other's love-needs to ensure the success of their marriage. Hence, the civil authorities who endorse and legally authenticate marriages in various nations or states serve as witness reminder to the spouses of their own voluntary love-need vow responsibilities to each other for a lifetime.

4. CHURCH WITNESS OF THE MARITAL LOVE-NEED VOW REMINDER

The church also serves as a witness reminder for spouses who marry in the church. Usually, the churches may assign couples to counseling with the expectation of equipping them to help set their success and happiness stage for their marriage. Couples who include the church in the process of their marriage should also see the church as a witness reminder of their own love-need vow responsibilities to each other for their lifetime.

5. FRIENDS WITNESS OF MARITAL LOVE-NEED VOW REMINDER

Lastly, couples should not just be happy to see their friends attending their marriages to celebrate with them. However, the couple must realize that friends are a reminder of their vow responsibilities to meet the love-needs of each other for their lifetime. The truth of the matter is that all the witnesses listed above, always hope, and pray to see the spouses enjoy the best of marriage for the rest of their lives. Hence, spouses should remember that all the five witness entities or groups are the reminder of their own vow responsibilities to meet the love-needs of each other for lifetime.

Marital love-need vow fulfillment is indispensable to the happiness and success of every marriage. Failure to fulfill them is a blatant refusal to enjoy marriage with its benefits. There should be no circumstance by which anyone should be blamed outside marriage for the unsuccessfulness of a marriage. If a marriage fails, the only people to be blamed are the spouses.

The scriptures say that people perish for lack of knowledge **(Hosea 4:6; paraphrased).** The scriptures again re-emphasize that *where there is no vision, the people perish: but he that keepeth the law, happy is he* **(Proverbs 29:18 KJV).** It is therefore, required of all those who desire to marry to seek the needed knowledge and should develop the willingness and commitment to apply its principles to ensure the success of their own marriage.

CHAPTER FOUR

THE ALONENESS AND LONELINESS PROBLEMS AND SOLUTIONS

*And the LORD God said, "It is not good that man should **be alone**; I will make him a **helper comparable to him**." [20] So Adam gave names to all cattle, to the birds of the air, and to every beast of the field. But for **Adam there was not found a helper comparable to him*** (**Genesis 2:18, 20**)

Aloneness Problem

… It is not good that man should be alone…

First and foremost, it was God Himself who saw the need to alleviate aloneness problem with its hidden loneliness problem from man's life. Aloneness of Adam means, he was by himself (alone). Adam's aloneness indicates the lack of a suitable or rightly fitted relationship support and friendship he desperately needed. In fact, there were different kinds of animals, and yet none was a good fit to meet Adam's physical and emotional needs.

God designed Adam in His image and likeness and yet he was different because he was a spirit housed in a physical body with five senses to appreciate and enjoy his world. This kind of human nature required both the spiritual and the physical connections for Adam to be fulfilled. God was fulfilling Adam's spiritual needs, but his physical needs were lacking fulfillment. Although, God paid regular visits to Adam in the evenings at *cool of the day* **(Genesis 3:8)**, and yet His presence could not suffice as the suitable fit for the kind of physical relationship He intended for Adam.

Divine Aloneness Solution

...I will make him a helper comparable to him **(Genesis 2:18).**

God's solution to Adam's aloneness problem was to provide him with a heterosexual person of his likeness to meet his human crying needs of friendship, partnership, complementarity, attention, one-fleshness of sex and the confidant of trust. God's intended purposes of marriage as indicated in the are many. However, this principle is just to explain the divine solution of the aloneness problem in human life.

The statement, the *"helper comparable to him"* is a vice versa statement, meaning Adam, who was the potential husband, was created with indispensable needs which required another heterosexual being to fulfill them for him. Eve, on the other hand as the potential wife was also created with indispensable needs, which required fulfillment from Adam her potential husband.

Adam and Eve as the first spouses were brought together by God in marriage to give attention to their various needs by ensuring their own happiness and success in the marriage. The fulfilling of spousal needs is reciprocal, requiring mutual attention from each other. The moment selfishness and self-centeredness set in, negative emotions of disappointment, hurt, anger and other such subsequent ones get aroused to trouble the marital relationship. The caution then is that meeting of needs in marriage should never become one sided love responsibility. The rationale is that one-sidedness of marital love-need fulfillment is a violation of marital mutual reciprocity which ensures success of marriage and happiness of each other.

Marital indispensable or crying needs, therefore, require mutual reciprocal meeting of each other's needs. God required Eve to provide Adam with the help he desperately needed. By the principle of reciprocity of exchanging or giving and receiving, God required Adam to enjoy Eve's help by meeting her needs in return.

Again, God required Adam to receive Eve as his very bone of bones and flesh of his flesh by offering to her the needed love of affection. By the same principle of reciprocity, Eve was also required by God to receive Adam as her very bone of bones and flesh of her flesh by offering him his needed love of respect. Spouses must therefore, secure their own happiness in the marriage by committing to their vows to meet each other's needs. The meeting of each other's needs as spouses should not be a nine-day wonder but must be practiced throughout lifetime. Consequently, aloneness is usually likely to lead to loneliness and loneliness is liable to lead to emotional hurts to start causing marital troubles.

Loneliness Problem

...But for Adam there was not found a helper comparable to him (**Genesis 2:20**).

Loneliness on the other hand is caused by the lack of willingness from each spouse to meet each other's mental, emotional, and physical needs. Spouses by their own love-need vows require them to meet each other's needs in the areas of friendship, partnership, care, communication, empathy, romance, intimacy, trust, and security.

Adam's aloneness generated loneliness because there was no one with a nature like him to provide the needed relationship and help his soul was yearning for as stated above. Again, whereas, aloneness is a state or physical condition, loneliness is an emotional hunger caused by unmet emotional needs which adversely affect the mental well-being of a person.

One of the debilitating problems with some marriages is that the spouses are surely not alone because they live in the same home, and sleep on the same bed every day, and yet feel lonely. The cause for such marital loneliness is resulted from the neglect of each other's indispensable emotional, mental, and physical needs of attention, support, romance, intimacy, trust, and security.

The fulfillment of each other's emotional needs is necessary to the wellbeing of each spouse. For this reason, spouses are required by their own love-vows to meet each other's indispensable needs which ensures one's own happiness. Meeting each other's marital needs as spouses is indispensable to the health and success of all marriages. In other words, no marriage can succeed without the fulfilment of each other's emotional, mental, and physical needs. The focus must then be to pledge marital love to a person with the intention and commitment to meet their needs by way of ensuring the fulfillment of your own needs.

Divine Loneliness Solution

> *Then the rib which the LORD God had taken from man He made into a woman, and He brought her to the man*
> **(Genesis 2:22)**

The God who created man with the in toto understanding of his makeup and what to make him fulfilled, created a suitable solution from him to him. In other words, God took a live rib of connection from Adam to create a suitable woman for him. The reason was that there was no one from all God's creation to fulfill the needs of Adam.

Therefore, God instituted marriage by given Adam a suitable and a lovely wife whom he acknowledged as one who shared things in common with him. In a sense, the woman who was created with the element of her husband in her was required to meet her husband's love-needs to alleviate his loneliness whiles at the same time alleviating her own loneliness.

Adam who was so motivated by love admitted that she was indeed his *bone of bones and flesh of his flesh* (**Genesis 2:23**). He even went further to give her a name, "woman" as an acknowledgement of her feminine needs as a wife with the willingness and readiness to meet those needs for her. Adam even vowed to meet her needs with the same statement: You are …*now bone of my bones and flesh of my flesh; you shall be called woman, because you were taken out of me* (**Genesis 2:23**).

When Adam made this vow to his wife Eve, he was admitting that all the good things he would desire and want for himself, he was willing and ready to give to her as also indicated in **Ephesians 5:28-29:** *So, husbands ought to love their own wives as their own bodies; he who loves his wife loves himself. For no one ever hated his own flesh, but nourishes and cherishes it, just as the Lord does the church*. Even though, God has instituted marriage to provided solution to spouses' loneliness, and yet, husbands and wives still experience the loneliness problems despite living together.

The only reason for this kind of frustration in marriage is as a resulted from the neglect of each other's love-vows to fulfill each other's love-needs. Loneliness in marriage is affecting and frustrating so many marriages all around the world. Spouses must therefore, pay attention to each other's unique needs respectively as a husband and a wife. The commitment to fulfill each other's love needs is what ensures the happiness of each other and the success of the marriage. The caution then states: *Therefore, "let nothing be done **through selfish ambition or conceit**, but in **lowliness of mind** let each **esteem others better than himself**. ⁴Let each of you **look out not only for his own interests**, but also **for the interests of others** (Philippians 2:3-4)."*

CHAPTER FIVE

MARITAL AGREEMENT NEEDS PRINCIPLES

Can two walk together without agreeing to meet?
(Amos 3:3, CSB)

Agreement is universal to any group venture or partnership, and it is even required of individuals agreeing with themselves to generate confidence to undertake certain ventures of life. There is no partnership that can work successfully without agreeing to abide by the same rules of purpose, goals, and security. Hence, agreement in the context of marriage is indispensable to agreement of compatibility which ensures a walk in the same direction, leading to success and greater achievable results. Marital compatibility of agreement is not an automatic flow of agreement but rather, it is the willingness to commit to the same rules of love, purpose, partnership, investment, goals, and security.

Agreement in marriage, is the process which leads to compatibility requiring willingness, knowledge, understanding, commitment, selflessness, and self-adjustment efforts to bring about agreement and success in marriage. The compatibility test for relationships is designed to help couples to determine whether the intended person for relationship or marriage is a good fit. However, even if the test proves a couple to be a good fit, it can neither assure the success of the marriage nor the happiness of each other. Agreement in marriage is an intentional, consistent, and committed work efforts to ensure compatibility among spouses.

Agreement of compatibility is made possible through consistent and committed self-adjustment efforts with other requirements stated above. Adjustment, however, is the process of adapting to new life of the marriage, the altering of old perspectives and habits of life, and becoming used to the new lifestyle of the marriage. By doing so, the spouses are sure to achieve their desired agreement, happiness, peace, harmony, commonness, understanding, and friendship.

Spouses must, therefore, be ready to move their marriage from the starting point of partial compatibility to the process of committed and consistent self-adjustments which aim toward the pleasing and making each other happy for lifetime. The pleasing of each other in the right way is sure to ensure the flow of compatibility of the harmonious, peaceful, and loving agreement among the spouses. Spouses must therefore commit to know and adjust to bring agreement from all their differences in areas such as: perceptions, gender need differences, temperaments, family orientations, preferences, status, culture, education, finances, religion, work, and various exposures of life.

The question then is, how well and committed can the spouses adjust to bridge the gaps of differences without allowing them to cause confusion and separation in their marriage? Marital agreement of compatibility, therefore, requires the process of conscious and continuous commitment to adjust one's own self-interests in order to embrace the mutual interests for the purpose and success of the marriage. Hence, the focus of each spouse should be about serving the mutual interests of the marriage, but not their own interest in order to start the life process of compatibility. Before a couple agrees to marry, they should have already agreed to go their marital journey on the same direction and toward the same destination of fulfillment, being motivated by love.

If the spouses neglect the requirements of the marital agreement with any selfish or self-centered motivations, marital agreement of compatibility is compromised to generate confusion and conflicts. Furthermore, if the marital path splits to any direction other than the agreed direction, each spouse shall keep going in the marital journey without ever meeting by way of agreement. When this happens in marriage, it shall lead to irresolvable conflicts, and subsequent loss of each other.

The agreement of marital compatibility can only be possible through continuous commitment to self-adjustments. Continuous self-adjustments shall produce the benefits of success and imaginable happiness the spouses desire to experience. For spouses to agree and harmonize their differences in the areas of perceptions, gender, temperaments, family orientations, preferences, status, culture, education, finances, religion, work, and various exposures of life, they have to commit to adjust in these ten required areas listed below:

1. Spouses must commit to the adjustment of agreement by living by the same standards, values, purpose, and goals.

2. Spouses must commit to the adjustment of agreement by acknowledging the principles of togetherness, equalness and commonness, thereby, having all things in common in sharing of thoughts, ideas, interests, privileges, and ownership for mutual benefit.

3. Spouses must commit to the adjustment of agreement by appreciating each other's strengths and uniqueness, and at the same time tolerating and helping each other to work on weaknesses without feeling criticized, condescended, or looked down upon.

4. Spouses must commit to the adjustment of agreement to show loving empathy toward each other's problems as one's own.

The Need-Vow Responsibilities of Marriage

5. Spouses must commit to the adjustment of agreement to express love actions to each other without excuses.

6. Spouses must commit to the adjustment of agreement by keeping in focus the mutual interests of the marriage.

7. Spouses must commit to the adjustment of agreement to be on the same page in all matters of the marriage. Marriage should not be like a mastermind game whereby, one person sets the code, and the other partner seeks to break the code. Moreover, marriage must not be a secret coding whereby spouses hide things from each other and make decisions without involving the other. Rather, marriage must be mutual in all spousal endeavors.

8. Spouses must commit to the adjustment of agreement for each other to acknowledge their own weaknesses, mistakes, and wrongs. The spouses should accept responsibility for their own mistakes or wrongs, apologize and correct their own actions promptly to safeguard each other's emotions. Spouses must always be ready to forgive and receive forgiveness.

9. Spouses must commit to the adjustment of agreement by putting in all the required efforts to unite by ensuring their own happiness and success. Unity

is not just the absence of conflict or disagreement, but it is the intentional unanimous agreement to undertake an agreed course of action to fulfill the common purpose of the marriage. What then is effort? It is an intentional exertion of mental, emotional, volitional, and physical energies into a desired action plan that ensures accomplishments or achievements as affirmed: *Make every effort to keep the unity of the Spirit through the bond of peace* (**Ephesians 4:3**).

Again, the spouses can ensure their own unity by combining their efforts to see to the cleaving or sticking together of their minds, emotions, volitions of decisions, conscience of right and wrongs, intuitions of ideas and innovations, and physical strengths and senses to fulfill the common purpose of the marriage. Unity in marriage serves as the supportive system for the spouses' emotions and it must, therefore, be seen as a priority for the marital success and happiness. Marital unity at this level of agreement shall yield greater results and benefits that can be mutually enjoyed by the spouses for their lifetime.

10. Spouses must commit to the adjustment of agreement by ensuring marital bond of peace through the sacrificing of their ego of selfishness, self-centeredness, and pride to promote the expected marital harmony. Spouses must see to it that all what they think, say, and do should be about peace and

not things that arouse unnecessary tensions and disagreements. Hence, spouses must put in all the efforts to selflessly agree in every way possible by prioritizing and emphasizing peace in their marriage.

PART TWO

COMPREHENSIVE BIBLICAL DEFINITION OF MARRIAGE WITH ITS SEVENTEEN PRINCIPLES

CHAPTER ONE

COMPREHENSIVE BIBLICAL MEANING OF MARRIAGE

First and foremost, it is extremely important to define what the subject of marriage really is in order to ascertain its real essence and requirements to ensure the proper building of its foundation, pillars, and its projected structure of beauty. A poorly defined subject always results in poor understanding and wrong perception, leading to wrong application and subsequent life of jeopardy and failure.

The meaning of marriage to be treated in this chapter is a comprehensive one from a biblical perspective. It is an encompassing meaning, which consists of seventeen foundational marital principles. The seventeen principles which are connotated in the meaning of marriage below are guides to help spouses construct or reconstruct the right foundation, erect the right pillars, and build the right structure of marital success and happiness.

Marriage Defined

Marriage is a binding-lifelong, mutual life development, needs fulfillment, and betterment covenant between a man and a woman who have conscientiously decided to share their love, and lives; sacrifice their rights to control, self-pleasing, privacy, and comfortability to fulfill each other's happiness, self-worth, and security for better and for worse times as husband and wife.

CHAPTER TWO

SEVENTEEN PRINCIPLES OF THE MEANING OF MARRIAGE

1) Marriage is a binding-lifelong, 2) mutual life development, 3) needs fulfillment, and 4) betterment covenant, 5) between a man and a woman 6) who have conscientiously decided to share their love, and 7) lives, 8) sacrifice their rights to control, 9) self-pleasing, 10) privacy, and 11) comfortability 12) to fulfill each other's happiness, 13) self-worth, and 14) security 15) for better and for worse times 16) as husband and 17) wife.

1. Marriage is a Binding-Lifelong Covenant

Marriage is a binding-lifelong covenant. Marital covenant can be defined as a voluntary union between a man and a woman of their self-commitment binding pledge to meet each other's love-needs for a lifetime. Marriage by God's design is a voluntary vow agreement between a man and a woman for the partnership of common purpose to fulfill each other's love-needs for a lifetime. Lifelong or lifetime marriage requires lifetime responsibility of love commitment, endurance, and security of future certainties. However, the caution then is this, no one should contract marriage with the trifle mentality or attitude of trying it out. The reason is that marriage is your life worth and the life of another and therefore, should not be treated with the venture of luck or trial and error to harm the life of another.

It is incumbent on all spouses to seek knowledge and develop the right understanding of marriage, if they really want to enjoy its full benefits, because *for lack of knowledge people perish…* **(paraphrased from Hosea 4:6).** If your intention of marrying is for a short term, then marriage is not for you; and if you persist to venture it, you have indeed positioned yourself to hurt an innocent person. The point of reasoning here is that right from the word go, you have stifled the success of the marriage with such a trifling or trivialized mindset. Anyone who decides to marry, must understand that their own happiness is dependent on their own continuous commitment to meet each other's needs for a lifetime and not for some time.

2. Marriage is a Mutual Life Development Covenant

Marriage requires an unflinching goal of both spouses to develop each other to the desired best, being motivated by the patience of love. No one is perfect; hence, marriage creates the opportunity and the responsibility to help develop each other to become a suitable partner by submitting and adjusting to each other willingly and committedly.

Marriage by purpose is goal-oriented to empower each spouse to mature, progress, flourish and excel in all good things in the marital relationship for the holistic benefit of each other. Spouses by marital default, supposed to become each other's helper and each other's bone of bones and flesh of their own flesh. If spouses would remind themselves to develop and treat each other as their own self, no one in marriage shall lack any good thing because *…no one ever hated his own flesh, but nourishes and cherishes it, just as the Lord does the church* (**Ephesians 5:29**).

3. Marriage is Needs Fulfillment Covenant

Marriage is needs fulfillment covenant. Marriage authenticates the solemn pledge of the spouses to fulfill each other's needs by communicating love, respect, admiration, friendship, support, trust, and security with each other. The central responsibility of marriage is to meet each other's needs to ensure marital happiness and success. Needs fulfillment is very central to the duties of marriage, whereby, each spouse is required to pledge their commitment to meet each other's needs without negligence or excuses. The major cause of marital conflicts and confusion is mostly resulted from the neglect of each other's love-need vow responsibilities to each other.

The love-need vows of spouses make them responsible for the happiness and satisfaction of each other's emotional and physical needs. The continuous neglect of the satisfying of each other's needs shall surely arouse negative emotions of disappointment, hurts, bitterness, and anger. Hence, spouses' commitment to their covenant responsibility to fulfil each other's needs is crucial to their own happiness and success of the marriage.

4. Marriage is a Betterment Covenant

Marriage is a betterment covenant. Marriage requires each spouse's pledge of commitment to make each other better as spouses. The ultimate question spouses need to ask themselves as a guide toward making each other into a better person is this; what can I do or add to my spouse's life to ensure their happiness, beauty, prosperity, security and to motivate their integrity? It must be the responsibility of each spouse to develop a consistent daily thought of figuring out what each can do to bring about emotional health, mental health, physical health, beauty, and prosperity to each other.

Spouses must therefore, conscientize themselves with the fact that marriage is not about oneself. Rather, it is about each other's spouse's betterment and in doing so, one's own betterment becomes fulfilled or satisfied. The moment the marital betterment attention shifts from each other to self, the ego of selfishness, self-centeredness, and pride becomes the offensive language and practice to hurt each other.

The Scriptures cautions against this egoistic attitude in these words: *Let each of you look out **not only for his own interests**, but also **for the interests of others*** **(Philippians 2:4).** Spouses must, therefore, aim at always making each other the focus of attention in the journey of the marriage to ensure each other's betterment and happiness.

5. Marriage is Between a Man and a Woman

Marriage was instituted by God to be between a man and a woman. It must be realized that God from the beginning of creation, intended marriage to be heterosexual to fulfill unique marital and life love-needs as follows: The first unique fulfillment is complementarity which makes each other complete; and the second fulfills the continuous procreation and posterities. The man and the woman were both created in God's image to fulfill each other's needs uniquely, and to continue the posterity of the human race as affirmed: *So, God created man in His own image; in the image of God, He created him; male and female He created them. ²⁸ Then God blessed them, and God said to them, "Be fruitful and multiply; fill the earth and subdue it; have dominion over the fish of the sea, over the birds of the air, and over every living thing that moves on the earth* **(Genesis 1:27-28)."**

The God who created mankind and instituted marriage from the very beginning of life, intended it to be heterosexual, thus, between a man and woman. Any other definition or reinvention of marriage would be considered by God as a perversion of His original plan, or intent of what is right and acceptable in His sight.

The building of right and true foundation for all life endeavors is a prerequisite to the success of all life's endeavors. To experience the best of life, one needs to understand its requirements, and operations and must be willing to apply its principles to enjoy its fruit. Spouses should not allow the challenges of their marriage to motivate them to choose for an alternative lifestyle, because it is not the answer to their problem. Understanding marriage, developing the willingness, and the commitment to apply its love-need vow principles are the key to its enjoyment, no matter the differences in life's orientations, experiences, and culture.

6. Marriage is a Conscientious Decision to Share Each Other's Love

Marriage is a conscientious or carefully thought-out decision to share each other's love. Each spouse is entitled to each other's love without to beg for it. To marry is to have a carefully thought-out decision to love your wife by fulfilling the crying need of her love of affection. The wife's ultimate need of the love of affection includes but not limited to the enjoyment of the good feelings of endearment, self-worth, belovedness, beauty, belonging, honor, happiness, pleasure, protectiveness, and future security from her husband. In matters of facts, it is only the husband who can make his wife into the happy, fulfilled, beautiful, confident, exclusive significant partner and homemaker he expects.

The wife by the same token is also required by her own carefully thought-out vow decision to submit to her own husband by fulfilling his ultimate love-need of respect of his person and leadership in the marital home. Respecting the person of the husband comprises but not limited to the respect of his intellect of opinions, emotions, volitions of mutual decisions, conscience of right and wrongs, and intuition of his ideas. If the wife refuses to express her love of respect toward her husband by acknowledging him as the servant leader of their home, she will render him impotent and less useful in her life and in their home. It is only the wife who can make her own husband into the real confident and responsible man she expects by expressing her love of respect to him with regards to his personhood and leadership.

7. Marriage is a Conscientious Decision to Share each Other's Life.

Again, marriage is a conscientious or carefully thought-out decision to share each other's life's energies and prospects for the benefit and progress of the marriage in six major ways: First, spouses must commit to share their mental energies of knowledge, wisdom, understanding, expertise, and other natural unique perceptivities and potentials to enrich and prosper their present and future lives.

In life's natural perceptivities, the average man perceives life from far-to-near, whereas the average woman perceives life from near-to-far. Hence, the advantages of the heterosexual perceptivity are sure to guarantee a better understanding of their present circumstances and the prospects of their marriage. African adage affirms that "two heads are better than one." In a marital relationship, two heads are indeed better than one for a promising future. The reason is that the two heterosexual unique spouses can better understand the present to envision and plan for the future prosperity of the marriage.

Second, spouses must commit to share their emotional energies. Emotional energies can be shared in two ways:

1. Spouses share in their emotional energies by refraining from selfish, self-centered, and arrogant motivations which arouse negative emotional feelings of fear, loneliness, sadness, annoyance, bitterness, discouragement, anger, and condescension in each other.
2. Spouses share in their emotional energies by intentionally arousing positive or healthy emotions such as endearment, closeness, admiration, happiness, trust, contentment, and security in each other.
3. Spouses share in their emotional energies through empathetic listening and supportive assistance.

Third, spouses must commit to serve each other with their volitional energy of the will power of decision. When spouses, show respect to each's inputs in all matters and decisions of life of the marriage with regards to their mutual lives, success and happiness shall be the song of marriage. Marital collectiveness of decision generates a powerful force for greater achievements and results.

Fourth, spouses must commit to share their intuitive energies by teaching and utilizing each other's unlearned known ideas to advice their future ventures. Unlearned known ideas are generated from the intuition which is located in the human spirit which can be termed as "the center of divine library of wisdom". General life solutions of the uncountable life problems which were not taught in the classrooms, originate from the intuition. Intuition serves as the library of wisdom in the spirit of all humanity.

Intuition supplies solution ideas for life' problems, questions or puzzles which is not known or taught in the classroom. If spouses would share and apply their intuitive ideas appropriately, their marriage has already projected itself into a brighter and a promising future. Spouses, should therefore, submit to each other by embracing, evaluating, owning, and utilizing each other's ideas for the prosperity of the marriage.

Fifth, spouses must not forget to share their conscience energies. Conscience deals with the innate knowledge of rights and wrongs with its corresponding emotional reactions. Right actions arouse peace and happiness within the person and the relationship. Whereas wrong actions arouse emotional tensions of the loss of peace and happiness in the relationship, which require immediate life amends.

Sharing and serving your spouse with the conscience, requires the spouses to be sensitive and considerate toward each other's emotions. Spouses' conscience must prompt them of their own offensive utterances or actions, and they must be prompted to apologize and make amends as quickly as possible.

The conscience again is the voice of our own spirit, and many can attest to its operation with this statement, "something told me, or something prompted me." All these promptings are from the conscience. The conscience promptings must be utilized to do the right things right at the right time with the right motive, being motivated by love toward each other as spouses, besides the application of the rightness you both know already.

Hence, spouses must share their conscience energies by being reflective of their thoughts before acting. Spouse must listen and evaluate the promptings of their conscience before acting to safeguard each other's emotions. Again, when spouses offend each other, they should not underestimate its seriousness and consequences because it will not only affect the offended but also the offender. Spouses must, therefore, be quick to admit faults, apologize and make amends. They must also do well to be sensitive and cautious toward each other's emotions in order not to arouse negative feelings irresponsibly.

Sixth, spouses must not forget to decisively share and serve each other with their physical energies of strength, skill sets, romance, and intimacy in every possible way as a proof of their love for each other. The spousal love for each other must always compel and motivate them to give the best out of their physical strengths, skill sets, romance, and intimacy to serve each other cheerfully.

8. Marriage is a Conscientious Decision to Sacrifice Rights to Control

Marriage is a conscientious decision to sacrifice rights to control. Sadly enough, so many people marry without understanding its undergirding love-need vow requirement of sacrifice. Sacrifice in marriage deals with losing what is dear to enjoy in order to focus on what produces the best for the marriage. Anyone, who truly marries with the intention to enjoy marriage must understand its principle of sacrifice. Sacrifice is the commitment to intentionally lose or forgo something particularly important in order to meet a need or requirement which later brings satisfaction and yields greater results.

Marriage requires the couple's conscientious or carefully thought-out voluntary decision to sacrifice their personal rights to control or authority to ensure each other's love-need fulfillments. Sacrificing rights in marriage is not an option but a requirement for those who want to enjoy the good things marriage has to offer to the spouses. Consequentially, the covenant of marriage requires each spouse to give up or bequeath their rights to control or authority over their own lives and body to their spouse. If a couple marries without the knowledge or understanding of the indispensable need of sacrifice to bequeath their rights of authority or control to their spouse, the marriage has been preset for future crisis.

After marriage, the innate authority everyone possesses to do what pleases self is voluntarily waived to give way for pleasing each other. Therefore, spouses must be willing to let go of their negative ego, of selfishness, self-centeredness, pride, and greed. The single life by default creates selfishness and self-centeredness. If spouses refuse to forgo their own ego, they will only be in the marriage to please and serve themselves and that will not augur well for the marriage. The ego of selfishness, self-centeredness, pride, and greed in marriage is always bound to neglect the love-need vow responsibility to love, uphold, serve, and respect each other.

Every spouse must acknowledge that after marriage, he or she has relinquished their own rights of control or authority to each other over your own body, time, decision, and personal preferences. In other words, after marriage, each spouse has received the full right over each other's total life. In this case, the spouses themselves have authorized each other to have a total say and influence over the life of each other. The Bible affirms the required sacrifice of rights to personal authority and control in these words: *The wife does not have authority over her own body, but the husband does. And likewise, the husband does not have authority over his own body, but the wife does* (**1 Cororintians 7:4**).

9. Marriage is a Conscientious Decision to Sacrifice Rights to Self-Pleasing

Marriage requires a careful thought-out decision to sacrifice or waive each other's right to self-pleasing or self-pleasure. In other words, marriage obligates the spouses to voluntarily commit to intentionally please each other by fulfilling each other's spouses' crying love-needs to the best of each other's ability for a lifetime. If couples marry to please and serve their own interests and agenda to the neglect of the marital purpose and interest, they have violated the foundational love-need principle of marriage.

Getting married with the intention to please self and serve one's own agenda is detrimental to marital success and happiness. In effect, it is a sowing of the seed of selfishness, self-centeredness and pride which will eventually arouse so many negative emotions to toxify the marital relationship. Anyone with a serious mind to marry and having the intention to enjoy marriage, should commit to sacrificing their rights to self-pleasing to give way to pleasing one's own spouse. In this case, an individual spouse shifts pleasing and pleasuring attention from self to their significant spouse.

10. Marriage is a Conscientious Decision to Sacrifice Rights to Privacy

Marriage by its foundational principle, requires the spouses to make a conscientious decision to voluntarily sacrifice their rights to privacy to each other. In other words, spouses must come to the high place of understanding and realization that each spouse has voluntarily sacrificed their own rights to privacy after marriage. Hence, each spouse is entitled to the absolute rights of honesty, transparency, and predictability of each other.

In the principle of sacrifice of rights to privacy, lies and secrecy should neither be practiced nor become a concern for loving spouses. Marriage requires the spouses to vacate their rights by granting each spouse the total right to the full knowledge of each other's life, emotions, and thoughts. The principle of losing each other's right to privacy also means that spouses are not supposed to feel intruded by their own spouse in any way or form. The Scriptures affirm this principle with these words: *"Therefore, whatever you want men to do to you, do also to them, for this is the Law and the Prophets* **(Matthew 7:12).**

Furthermore, if spouses cannot be an open book for each other, the marriage has been denied of the trust of reliance, confidence, and friendship. Spouses with genuineness of mind should not just become partners but should become close friends or confidants of trust as emphasized by our Lord Jesus; *"No longer do I call you servants, for a servant does not know what his master is doing; but I have called you **friends**, for **all things that I heard from My Father I have made known to you*** **(John 15:15).** Spouses should, therefore, give way to openness to the extent of allowing each spouse to predict what each other thinks and might do. This is called the openness of predictability. The openness of predictability should, therefore, be the bedrock of trust of reliance, confidence, and confidant-friendship in marriage.

11. Marriage is a Conscientious Decision to Sacrifice Rights to Comfortability

Furthermore, marriage requires the spouses to make

a conscientious decision to sacrifice their rights to comfortability. Candidates of marriage should understand that their decision to marry requires them to make a carefully thought-out decision to sacrifice their rights to their own comfortability in order to fulfill each other's love-need vow responsibilities to each other. Unfortunately, marriage brings an end to individual comfortability of preferences, freedom, and self-contentment. The self-centered attitude such as: "This is what I am used to" must give way to "this is what my spouse and I are used to or would love to do."

If a person marries and refuses to let go their "use to" of self-satisfying attitude, it will be difficult to fulfill each other's love-need vow responsibilities which bring satisfaction and happiness to each other. Before and after the marriage, the spouses must have understood that the life of the marriage is not about each other's comfortability of preferences, freedom, and self-contentment anymore. Rather, it is about what brings satisfaction and happiness to each other as spouses. It must, therefore, be the goal of every spouse to make each other comfortable, satisfied, and happy, and by doing so, each other's happiness becomes guaranteed.

12. Marriage is About Fulfilling Each Other's Happiness

Marriage is indeed about fulfilling each other's love-need to bring about happiness to each other. Happiness is based on favorable, positive, and pleasurable life circumstances and provisions. In effect, happiness is man-made in marriage because it is not an abstract thing which automatically happens to spouses. Rather, it requires the intentional creation of its atmosphere, conditions, and circumstances by each spouse in order for it to be enjoyed. Happiness in marriage is conditioned on the kind of emotions each spouse intentionally or unintentionally arouses in each other. In effect, to arouse negative emotions in your spouse without caution is an intentional way of snuffing out the blaze of happiness in the heart of your spouse.

Again, happiness in marriage is human made. The reason being that happiness in marriage is dependent on what each spouse says, does and gives or offers to each other with the intention to arouse happy feelings in each other. The royal law of love is based on reciprocity which requires two major love actions. In relations to marriage, the royal law requires that:

1. The kind of love each spouse nurtures for self, the same or more must be extended to the spouse they claim to love as affirmed: *If you really fulfill the* **royal law** *according to the Scripture,* **"you shall love your neighbor as yourself,"** *you do well* (**James 2:8**).

2. All the love and special treatment a spouse desires from each other, the same or more should be expressed toward each other as also affirmed: *"Therefore, whatever you want men to do to you, do also to them, for this is the Law and the Prophets* (**Matthew 7:12**).

The implication of this royal law or principle of love in marriage is that the key to the unlocking of each other's happiness is embedded in each other's spouse respectively. In this case, each spouse becomes the key to the happiness of each other. If both spouses commit to making each other happy, their present and future happiness is already assured and secured. The book of Philippians crowns this principle so beautifully in these words: **Fulfill my joy** *by being* **like-minded***, having the* **same love***, being of one accord, of one mind*. ³*Let nothing be done through* **selfish ambition or conceit***, but in* **lowliness of mind let each esteem others better than himself***.* ⁴*Let each of you look out* **not only for his own interests, but also for the interests of others** **(Philppians 2:2-4).**

13. Marriage is About Fulfilling Each Other's Self-Worth

Marriage by principle requires the spouses to affirm each other's self-worth. Self-worth or self-importance is a love-need, and it is fulfilled and affirmed through respecting and honoring of each other as spouses. In order words, marriage requires the spouses to intentionally engage in mutual respect and honor by the motivation of love.

Condescension of disrespect and general abuse of each other's person of intellect, emotions, and volitions, and physique in marriage are the devil's weapon which destroys each other's self-image of self-worth or self-esteem. First and foremost, the disrespect of your spouse's person of intellect refers to the downplaying of your spouse's mental capability to think, understand and apply wisdom. Second, the disrespect of your spouse's person of emotion implies to the insensitive and negligent attitude of arousing negative feelings in your spouse irresponsibly. And third, the disrespect of each other's spouse's person of volition signifies the making of decision without their inputs or the disregard of their inputs in the marital or personal decisions as marital partners.

Furthermore, the condescension of disrespect and abuse of each other's physique also deals with the refusal to appreciate each other's physical uniqueness and beauty. It also has to deal with making demeaning and derogatory statements about each other's body or physical appearance. Self-esteem is each other's self-confidence and emotional empowerment in marital relationship. Spouses must, therefore, do well to honor, respect and show admiration for each other to fulfill each other's self-worth for a lifetime.

14. Marriage is About Fulfilling Each Other's Security

Fulfilling marital security to each other in marriage deals with the spouses' commitment to protect each other from future disappointments and hurts. Firstly, the spousal security deals with protecting each other from irresponsible future emotional hurts and damages. Secondly, spousal security assures each other of present and future happiness and dependability. Thirdly, spousal security guarantees each spouse of a future being built together for mutual benefit and enjoyment.

Hence, spouses must commit to protect each other's emotions by respecting and meeting each other's love-needs for lifetime. Spouses again must commit to guarantee each other of a present and a future being built together for mutual benefit without future surprises and disappointments. It is in fact, the marital love-need vow duty of every spouse to give themselves every reason to trust each other completely. The trust of security is the way to protect the marriage from both inside and outside threats of disappointments and hurts. The security of trust in marriage assures each other of a present and future happiness and protection. Spouses by the motivation of their love-need vows are therefore required to commit to guarantee each other of a future being built for mutual benefit without outsmarting secrets and disappointments.

15. Marriage is About Fulfilling Each Other's Love-Needs in Both Better and Worse Times.

The love-need vows of marriage require the spouses to fulfill each other's love-needs in both better and worse times or convenient and inconvenient times throughout their marital journey. Life in general is unpredictable because anything can happen to anyone at any time without caution. When the unexpected happens, it begins to have a toll on each other. However, one of the benefits of marriage is that ...*two are better than one, because they have a good reward for their labor.* **¹⁰*For if they fall, one will lift up his companion. But woe to him who is alone when he falls, for he has no one to help him up*** (Ecclesiastes 4:9,10).

Spouses must, therefore, commit to assure each other against any present and future aloneness, loneliness, and disappointments. Spouses must prove their trust to each other by giving a total love assurance against future disappointments and mistreatments. Spouses are therefore required to prove their predictability and commitment by remaining faithful to hold to their end of the marital bargain. Spouses fulfill their marital love-need vow bargain by meeting each other's love-needs no matter the kind of time or life situation they found themselves. Spouses must do well to commit to meet each other's love-needs in both better and worse times. They must assure themselves with their unconditional love to remain lovingly supportive, dependable, and trustworthy, no matter the circumstances life may bring.

16. Marriage is About the Man Fulfilling His Responsibilities as a Husband.

In marriage, the man is not just a husband by name but a husband by responsibility. In other words, none of the names, husband and wife are just names or titles but they are an assignment or designated responsibilities in marriage. Therefore, husbands must assume their total responsibilities to their wives and to their children as fathers.

According to Merriam-Webster's Collegiate Dictionary, the word husband is from [4]"Old Norse, húsbóndi, from hús 'house' + bóndi householder, manger, steward.

---

4. Merriam-Webster, *Merriam-Webster's Collegiate Dictionary* (Springfield: Merriam-Webster,1998), 893.

Thus, to manage prudently and economically." By this definition, the husband supposed to be one who must hold the marital home together in the bond of peace and love. The husband is the steward who supposed to rightly manage his marital home, alongside his wife. The husband by responsibility is required to be a good servant leader who must assume full responsibility of his home by serving his wife and children as their servant leader.

Just as Christ has given up himself for his church, the husband is also required to do likewise as instructed: *Husbands, love your wives, just as Christ also loved the church and gave Himself for her* **(Ephesians 5:25)**. Again, just as Christ is the head of His church, the bride, so the husband is the head of his family as indicated: *For the husband is head of the wife, as also Christ is head of the church; and He is the Savior of the body* **(Ephesians 5:23)**. Moreover, just as Christ died to save and serve his church by giving Himself wholly to her, so the husband as the servant leader must also commit to take any risk for his wife and children no matter the circumstances.

The husband's leadership responsibility obligates him by God to be the responsible and the accountable one, who supposed to give himself fully in service to his wife and children by the motivation of love. Furthermore, the husband by the responsibility of his servant leadership and management of his home supposed to serve his wife and children in cheerfulness of love. Every husband should caution self not to relegate all the responsibilities of the home to his wife but should rather set an example of service in his home. Being an example of service is a great motivation for the wife to give and do her best for her husband and children as well.

God in His plan for the marital home, made the husband as the responsible one. God has also endowed the husband with a visionary ability to see life from far-to-near for the purpose of safeguarding him from being distracted in his leadership. The average husband can be described in his visionary abilities as the eagle which can see from an extremely far-to-near distances. On average, husbands can easily become preoccupied with a particular task and unintentionally neglect other areas in the marital home which may need his attention. That is why submission by way of listening and paying heed to each other as spouses becomes a key to good management of the marital home as affirmed: *...submitting to one another in the fear of God* **(Ephesians 5:21).**

17. Marriage is About the Woman Fulfilling Her Responsibilities as a Wife.

Women on the other hand must also assume their full responsibilities to their husbands as wives and to their children as mothers. In the principle of marriage, the woman is not just a wife by name but a wife by responsibility. The woman by virtue as a wife becomes her husband's significant partner who by marital responsibility is required to manage the home alongside her husband. The wife is endowed by God with unique capabilities to provide invaluable support to her husband and home which brings about beauty, peace, and order to her marital home for mutual enjoyment.

On average, wives have unique abilities to see life from near-to-far distances. This kind of ability is a plus for the husband and the marriage. The reason is that the wife shall not miss anything which requires immediate attention in the home. The average wife in her visionary abilities can be described as an owl which can turn its head around up to 360 and is also able to see clearly through the dark.

I quite remember some years past, my wife and I went to a place and after parking, we were walking to the place and I walked over a $50.00 bill without noticing, but my wife even saw it before I walked over it. After taking it, she exclaimed, "Dear, do you know you have just walked over a good money?" To my surprise, I had just walked over a $50 bill without seeing it. In fact, all my focus was at the destination and not what is on the road or the path.

The wife's near-to-far visionary abilities enables her to scan her environment at a glance to know what is lacking and what needs immediate attention. This is a key to making her a good homemaker. Although the husband can multitask, but the wife can do more of that and probably better as well. The good thing about the wife's unique abilities of seeing from near-to-far is that it enables her to know and give attention to anything which requires attention to turn the home into a place of beauty, plenty, rest, and safety. In other words, anything in the home which requires attentions shall never be missed by a diligent and a virtuous wife.

Additionally, Proverbs chapter 31 and verses 10-31 describe the good homemaking qualities of a virtuous wife who is considered as a morally sounded, disciplined or self-controlled and industrious. If wives would model after the qualities of the virtuous wife to assume their duties with their husbands, their life and home shall never lack any good thing. Interestingly enough, the qualities of the virtuous wife were taught and explained to king Lemuel by his own mother. There are at least seventeen virtuous qualities every wife must desire and make ready to model or apply to ensure order in the home and prosperity of their marriage:

The Sixteen Qualities of a Virtuous Wife (Proverbs 31:10-31)

1. The virtuous wife is invaluable to her husband and to her home because her qualities are indispensable to the success, prosperity and safety of her marriage and home as affirmed: ... *Who can find a virtuous wife? For her worth is far above rubies. (vs.10).*
2. The virtuous wife earns her trust by proving her undeniable and indisputable good deeds to her husband - *The heart of her husband safely trusts her; So, he will have no lack of gain. 12 She does him good and not evil all the days of her life. (vs.11-12).*
3. The virtuous wife is an income earner because she refuses to stay idle unless there is a halting reason or circumstances for it - *She seeks wool and flax, and willingly works with her hands. (vs.13).*
4. The home of a virtuous wife never lacks any good thing, and her home never runs short of food - *She*

is like the merchant ships, she brings her food from afar. 15 She also rises while it is yet night, and provides food for her household, and a portion for her maidservants. (vs. 14-15).

5. By application, the virtuous wife motivates her husband to jointly invest toward their future prosperity and enjoyment - *She considers a field and buys it; from her profits she plants a vineyard. (vs. 16).*
6. The virtuous wife is versatile, creative, and industrious in her home management duties - *She girds herself with strength and strengthens her arms. ^{18}She perceives that her merchandise is good, and her lamp does not go out by night. ^{19}She stretches out her hands to the distaff, and her hand holds the spindle. (vs. 17-19).*
7. By application, the virtuous wife encourages her husband toward liberality to the needy outside their family - *She extends her hand to the poor, yes, she reaches out her hands to the needy. (vs. 20).*
8. By application, the virtuous wife plans together with her husband for any seasons of life and also plan against the lack of any good thing for themselves and home - *She is not afraid of snow for her household, for all her household is clothed with scarlet. ^{22} She makes tapestry for herself; Her clothing is fine linen and purple. (vs. 21-22).*
9. The virtuous wife promotes her husband to the limelight and ensures his dignity and honor among dignitaries - *Her husband is known in the gates when he sits among the elders of the land. (vs. 23).*

10. The virtuous wife supports and shares her innovative or investment ideas with her husband and her husband gives her the success support she needs in their investments or business - *She makes linen garments and sells them and supplies sashes for the merchants (vs. 24)*.

11. The virtuous wife lives above reproach or dishonor - *Strength and honor are her clothing; she shall rejoice in time to come (vs. 25)*.

12. The virtuous wife exhibits respect in all her utterances and actions. Her lifestyle and utterances are governed by the law of respect, encouragement, and motivation. She knows what to say and how to say it at every given time of their lives - *She opens her mouth with wisdom, and on her tongue is the law of kindness (vs.26)*.

13. The virtuous wife knows whatever is lacking in her home and ensures their provision. No need goes unnoticed in her home because she is always on the lookout for the needs of her husband, children, and home - *She watches over the ways of her household and does not eat the bread of idleness (vs. 31:27)*.

14. The virtuous wife earns the respect and admiration of her husband and children - *Her children rise up and call her blessed; Her husband also, and he praises her:* [29]*"Many daughters have done well, but you excel them all." (vs. 28-29)*.

15. The virtuous wife fears God and as a result, she refuses to be influenced and strayed by her charms

and beauty. By her fear of God, the virtuous wife commits to hate sin, avoids all forms of evil and serves God by His standards; being motivated by genuine love, and reverence; being undergirded by the awareness of God's omniscience (all-knowingness), omnipresence (everywhere present), omnipotence (all-powerfulness) and God's justice that punishes sin but rewards righteousness - *Charm is deceitful and beauty is passing, but a woman who fears the LORD, she shall be praised. (vs. 30).*

16. The undeniable virtuous work and morals of the virtuous wife speak and testify about her in her home and public - *Give her of the fruit of her hands, and let her own works praise her in the gates. (vs. 31).*

PART THREE

LOVE DEFINITION WITH ITS THREE DIMENSIONS

Owe no one anything except to love one another, for he who loves another has fulfilled the law
(Romans 13:8).

General Expectational Love (GEL),
Multifunctional Applied Love (MAL)
Exclusive Reciprocal Obligatory Love (EROL)

CHAPTER ONE

MEANING OF LOVE

Love from the biblical perspective is the willingness, the commitment, the sacrifice, and the strong desire which drives a person to express or offer their best to another voluntarily to satisfy a need or a requirement. Love is quintessential to marriage because it is a virtue which presents high quality or an ideal moral set of values such as rightness, giving, sacrifice, kindness, loyalty, protection, trust, and mercy of forgiveness. The nature of God is love as affirmed: *He who does not love does not know God,* **for God is love** **(1John 4:8).** God created humans in His own image and likeness to love Him and love each other. However, sin has caused humanity to be egoistic, leading to the concentration of love on self alone. Love from its meaning above possesses the following qualities:

First, for love to be expressed voluntarily to satisfy a need or requirement, a person must develop the virtue of willingness to love. The rationale is that love by nature supposed to be freely given and freely received. It can neither be forced to be given nor be forced to receive. However, the principle of love requires that the willingness to receive love must correspond to the willingness to give or return love. To receive and enjoy love without the willingness to return love is a violation of love principle which shall eventually stifle the flow of love from being enjoyed.

Second, love from its meaning above supposed to be expressed out of commitment. In effect, the expression of love requires committed decision to express love to another voluntarily and genuinely. If the expression of love is only based on emotions, it will fluctuate on high, mid, low, and zero levels, which will make the giver of love inconsistent, unpredictable, and unreliable. Rather, love supposed to be based on commitment or on a decisive mind to express it no matter the convenient or the inconvenient circumstances.

Third, love from its required qualities supposed to be expressed not only on willingness and commitment alone but also on sacrifice. Sacrifice by definition is the understanding of a required cost of action with its intentional commitment to lose or forgo something particularly important or dear, in order to meet a need or requirement which later brings satisfaction or yields greater results. Hence, love without sacrifice cannot be termed as a genuine because it will fail and disappoint in the course.

Fourth, for love to be expressed passionately and joyfully, the person expressing love must have a strong desire to love. The strong desire of love serves as the drive or motivation to offer one's best to another person voluntarily to satisfy their need or meet a particular requirement of life.

The strong desire to express love is developed by willingness, commitment, and sacrifice which motivates a person to express or offer their best to a person voluntarily to meet their need or satisfy a requirement of life.

Love is indeed complex, deep, and versatile in its requirements and expressions. Love in its deeper meaning, requirements, dimensions, and expressions is not a one size fits-all. It is really diverse, its purposes different and requirements peculiar. In this part, I will briefly define the three love dimensions and lay the foundational principles for each as listed: General Expectational Love (GEL), Multifunctional Applied Love (MAL) and Exclusive Reciprocal Obligatory Love (EROL). However, I will only explore the Multifunctional Applied Love (MAL) more deeply and apply its principles more extensively for the purpose of this book. The other love dimensions shall be treated in detail in the near future.

CHAPTER TWO

THE GENERAL EXPECTATIONAL LOVE (GEL)

The General Expectational Love (GEL) is a love dimension which is common to all and needed or yearn for by every human being. It is the kind of love every human being desire to receive or experience. The General Expectational Love (GEL) dimension is expected by everyone; even those who hate others. It is the genuine love of respect, care, giving and protection that makes the receiver feel good, self-important, cared for, accepted, and secured.

The expression of the General Expectational love dimension makes its recipients feel fulfilled, accepted, and safe. When individuals or families fail to express the GEL to each other, it leaves them with confusion and dejection, which motivates all kinds of selfish ambitions and behaviors. The General Expectational Love is outlined and briefly explained in the first book of Corinthians chapter thirteen and verses one through eight as follows:

Though I speak with the tongues of men and of angels, but have not love, [1]have become sounding brass or a clanging cymbal. [2]And though I have the gift of prophecy, and understand all mysteries and all knowledge, and though I have all faith, so that I could remove mountains, but have not love, I am nothing. [3]And though I bestow all my goods to feed the poor, and though I give my body to be burned, but have not love, it profits me nothing. [4]**Love suffers long** *and* **is kind; love does not envy; love does not parade itself, is not puffed up;** [5]**does not behave rudely, does not seek its own, is not provoked, thinks no evil;** [6]**does not rejoice in iniquity,** *but* **rejoices in the truth;** [7]**bears all things, believes all things, hopes all things, endures all things.** [8]**Love never fails.** *But whether there are prophecies, they will fail; whether there are tongues, they will cease; whether there is knowledge, it will vanish away.*

CHAPTER THREE

THE MULTIFUNCTIONAL APPLIED LOVE (MAL)

The Multifunctional Applied Love (MAL) is the kind of love that can be applied to different kinds of relationships. What I term as Multifunctional Applied Love (MAL) is a dimension of love which is derived from the seven Greek forms of love. The seven Greek dimensions of love fulfills several functions and can be applied to various forms of relationships. In this book, the seven Multifunctional Applied Love dimension is tailored and applied into practical marriage expressions of love which is sure to ensure success and happiness in marriage.

The MAL dimension of love, when expressed in its entire seven forms in marriage, success, happiness, and security become a reality for spouses. Love is deep and very versatile in its application; and it is not like one size fits all as portrayed in our society now adays. The MAL dimensional principles with its details are applied to marital success and happiness in part six of chapter two of this book.

CHAPTER FOUR

THE EXCLUSIVE RECIPROCAL OBLIGATORY LOVE (EROL)

The Exclusive Reciprocal Obligatory Love (EROL) is the spousal reciprocal or mutual love obligation or responsibility. The EROL mutual or reciprocal love requires willingness, commitment, sacrifice, and a compelling desire to meet each other's needs of love for lifetime which ensures success and happiness in the marriage.

First, the EROL is exclusive; meaning, it is best applied in marriage between the husband and his wife. The exclusiveness of EROL limits its love expression among the spouses alone. The failure to confine the expression of this love to the marriage, violates the love-need vows security of each other as spouses.

Second, the EROL love expression in marriage is required to be reciprocal, which simply means that it is mutual and cannot be best applied one-sidedly. EROL love expression among spouses requires mutual correspondence from each other. If EROL is express from only one of the spouses, it will begin to create love imbalance of disappointment, hurts, and subsequent anger of chaos. The spouses who have truly married on the firm foundation of love must both commit to express EROL respectively and both spouses must also receive love from each other with gratitude.

Third, all marital needs as well as the Exclusive Reciprocal Obligatory Love (EROL) is obligatory as affirmed with this principle of mutual submission in these words, ... *Submitting yourselves one to another in the fear of God* (**Ephesian 5:21**). Thus, submitting to one another is the principle of mutual submission which is required in marital success and happiness. Mutual submission among spouses requires willingness and commitment to pleasing and fulfilling each other's love-needs. Hence, the expression of EROL in marriage is neither optional nor voluntary because the spouses' happiness and the success of the marriage are dependent on it. Spousal neglect of their own love-need vow responsibilities to each other has always been the cause of marital conflicts and heartbreaks.

Couples must understand that their decision to marry is not about putting together a beautiful wedding. Rather, it is about their willingness, commitment, sacrifice, and their compelling desire to fulfil each other's vow responsibilities to each other for a lifetime. The failure to meet this love-need vow responsibilities to each other as spouses arouse emotional hunger, which shall lead to marital imbalance of tension and confusion with time.

Therefore, by the principles of marriage, spouses must acknowledge that two people cannot achieve the mutual love goal without their genuine commitment to fulfill each other's love-need vow responsibilities. There are four Exclusive Reciprocal Obligatory Love by which all spouses who are anticipating marital success and happiness, should pay serious attention to, and commit to express to each other for lifetime.

PART FOUR

THE FOUR EXCLUSIVE RECIPROCAL OBLIGATORY LOVE (EROL)

- The Exclusive Reciprocal Obligatory Wife's Love-Need of Affection
- The Exclusive Reciprocal Obligatory Husband's Love-Need of Respect
- The Exclusive Reciprocal Obligatory Love of Romance
- Exclusive Reciprocal Obligatory Love of Intimacy

CHAPTER ONE

THE EXCLUSIVE RECIPROCAL OBLIGATORY WIFE'S LOVE-NEED OF AFFECTION

***Husbands, love your wives**, just as Christ also loved the church and gave Himself for her, [28]**So husbands ought to love their own wives as their own bodies; he who loves his wife loves himself**. [33]Nevertheless let each one of you in particular so **love his own wife as himself**, and let the wife see that she respects her husband* **(Ephesians 5:25, 28, 33).**

The Exclusive Reciprocal Obligatory wife's love-need of affection is the number one or the ultimate love-need every wife expect to be expressed regularly and consistently toward her by the husband. Every husband is required by the responsibility of the love-need vows of marriage to intentionally embark on expressing this special love-need throughout their lifetime toward their wives. If a husband neglects his wife's crying love-need to starve and to make her desperate to beg for it, he is nurturing bitterness to destroy her, himself, and the marriage.

The love of affection is the core love-need and the right of every wife as God intended it. The reason for this ultimate wife's love-need of affection is that she feeds on it for her emotional nourishment and mental soundness. The passage of scripture above requires husbands to love their wives as their own bodies and also to give themselves wholly to their wives as Christ did for His church. The required love of husbands from the above Scripture to be expressed toward their wives is the wives' love-need of affection. The wife's love-need of affection which is required of her husband is exclusive to her and cannot be shared with any other woman.

As already emphasized, the love of affection is every wife's crying need, and it requires a continuous obligatory attention from husbands. When this kind of love feels fulfilled in wives, it arouses good feelings of self-confidence, acceptance and great happiness which motivates them to offer their best to their husbands and marriage. In effect, if the Exclusive Reciprocal Obligatory love of affection is intentionally and continuously expressed toward a wife, she will always feel endeared, accepted, special, beautiful, confident, and admired.

Eve, the first wife, felt fully accepted and admired when her husband expressed his love of affection toward her with these words: *And Adam said: "This is now bone of my bones and flesh of my flesh; She shall be called woman, because she was taken out of Man* **(Genesis 2:23).***"* The husband's expression of his wife's need-based love of affection is what makes him attractive and irresistible to his wife.

What then is the exclusive wives' love-need of affection from the context of marriage? Marital affection refers to the pleasant things husbands by their love motivation say, do and give or offer to their wives intentionally which arouses in them the good feelings of endearment, care, admiration, beauty, confidence, belonging, pampering, honor, pleasure, happiness, safety, and security. Husbands should, therefore, have the thoughts of their wives in their minds always. They must ask themselves these three major following questions to aid them fulfill this ultimate crying love-need of affection toward their wives:

1. What should I, by the motivation of my love, **say** to arouse the good feelings of endearment, care, admiration, beauty, confidence, belonging, pampering, honor, pleasure, happiness, safety, and security in the heart and life of my wife?
2. What should I, by the motivation of my love, **do** to arouse the good feelings of endearment, care, admiration, beauty, confidence, belonging, pampering, honor, pleasure, happiness, safety, and security in the heart and life of my wife?

3. What should I, by the motivation of my love, **give or offer** to arouse the good feelings of endearment, care, admiration, beauty, confidence, belonging, pampering, honor, pleasure, happiness, safety, and security (present and future) in the heart and life of my wife?

The failure in commitment to accord the wife her need-based love of affection is to render her demoralized and wounded in the journey of the marriage, which in effect, slows down the success of the marriage and gradually impede the happiness of each other. When a husband refuses to satisfy his wife's crying love-need of affection, he has rendered her ineffective in operation as a wife.

When the wife becomes starved out of her love-need of affection, it demotivates and robs her of becoming the wife God intended her to be and the wife the husband expects her to be. Husbands should remember that psychologically, the emotions of women are inseparable from their minds and what affects their emotions positively or negatively also affects how they think and react concurrently. In fact, arousing negative emotions in your wife without caution is a way of causing her to function ineffectively as a wife which also affects the success of the marriage adversely.

Therefore, husbands must be more careful not to arouse their wives' negative emotions by refusing to fulfill their love-needs of affection; for such negligence shall not augur well for the success of the marriage. The Bible again, recommends to husbands to express the love-need of affection toward their wives and they are cautioned against the use of damaging utterances and behaviors toward their wives in these words: ***Husbands, love your wives** and do **not be bitter toward them*** **(Colossians 3:19).** First, it is recommended to husbands to meet their wives' love-needs of affection intentionally and continuously. Surprisingly, the love of affection is not just a need of a wife but rather, it is her right that must be received from the husband because she feeds on it for her mental and emotional nourishment. A wife may say, show me an unaffectionate and a demeaning husband and I will show you an undesirable husband.

Second, husbands are cautioned against the expression of bitter utterances and behaviors toward their wives. The bitter attitude, actions, and utterances of a husband toward his wife refers to the condescending or demeaning treatment of his wife. Expressing any bitter form of action is biblically and emotionally not recommended because it causes the wife to feel unloved, abused, disrespected, inferior, unattractive, and undeserving of the best and happiness of life from her husband. The bitter treatment of a wife does not only affects her negatively as a human, but it also affects the husband and the marriage negatively. Bitter treatments in marriage robs both spouses of their own happiness. Therefore, husbands, should do well to remember their own love-need vow duty to express the love of affection toward their wives intentionally and continually.

CHAPTER TWO

THE EXCLUSIVE RECIPROCAL OBLIGATORY HUSBAND'S LOVE-NEED OF RESPECT

Wives, submit to your own husbands**, as to the Lord. [23] For **the husband is head of the wife**, as also Christ is head of the church; and He is the Savior of the body. [24] Therefore, just as the **church is subject to Christ**, so **let the wives be to their own husbands in everything** [33] Nevertheless, let each one of you in particular so love his own wife as himself, and **let the wife see that she respects her husband **(Ephesians 5:22-24;33).**

The Exclusive Reciprocal Obligatory husband's love-need of respect is the number one love-need every husband expects from his wife. The scripture above obligates wives to submit to their own husbands ...*in everything* by way of meeting their love crying need of respect. The wife's required love of submission to her husband refers to her love of respect toward him as stated....*and let the wife see that she respects her husband*...In other words, wives are obligated by their own need-vow responsibilities of marriage to love their own husbands in everything through their submission of respect toward them in everything.

The major love-need which makes a husband feels fulfilled is his wife's willingness and commitment to meet his crying love need of respect. Thus, wives are required by the principles of marital love and vows to respect the personhood and leadership of their husbands in everything. Submission therefore should not be an intimidating word to wives. The reason is that submission in marriage has nothing to do with master and servant relationship. Rather it is about wives' required obligation to meet their husbands' crying love-need of respect as again stated... *and let the wife see that she respects her husband* (**Ephesians 5:33**).

The wife's core love expression which makes the husband feels loved and admired is her love of willing submission to meet his crying love-need of respect of his personhood and leadership as husband. The exclusive love-need of submission or respect is the wife's number one obligatory role toward her own husband. The wife's expression of respect to her husband is an indispensable need he can function without as a happy and effective husband. The love of respect is not just a need of a husband but rather, it is his right that must be received from the wife. The husband's love-need of respect is so important to him because he feeds on it for his mental and emotional nourishment.

Furthermore, the husband's exclusive reciprocal love-need of respect is what empowers him as a man and motivates him to be the effective leader, provider, and protector he ought to be for his wife, children, and home. The exhibition of wife's love of respect toward her own husband's personhood and leadership is what makes a her attractive and irresistible to her husband. A husband may say, show me a disrespectful and a demeaning wife and I will show you an unattractive wife.

The husband's love-need of respect of his personhood and leadership in the marriage is what empowers his self-esteem and challenges him to stand up to provide, protect and care for his family. If a wife robs her husband of this love-need of respect, she will in the course of time render him mentally, emotionally, volitionally, and physically ineffective and impotent. If a wife genuinely loves her husband, she will not find it difficult to acknowledge him and express her love of respect to his personhood and leadership.

Denying husbands of their love-need of respect of their personhood and servant leadership in the marriage is detrimental to the happiness of the spouses and the success of the marriage. This is because, depriving a husband of his love-need of respect does not only render him ineffective, irresponsible, and impotent, but it also renders him incapable of becoming the husband God intended him to be and the husband the wife expects him to be. Wives should not forget that psychologically, the mind and the emotions of husbands can easily be compartmentalized to affect their decisions and how they react. It is easy for a husband to choose to operate either with his emotions or mind. The best of a man and a husband a wife may want to have is the husband who positively operates with his mind and emotions concurrently toward his wife.

If the wife decides to fulfill her husband's love-need of respect, she will be able to positively impact the totality of his soul of mind, emotions, and volition toward positive decisions and actions. Again, when the wife lovingly and cheerfully begins to fulfill her love-need vow responsibility of respect toward her husband, she has already aroused the tripartite powers of his mind, emotions, and volition toward love and pleasurable actions.

The question then is, what does love of respect with regards to the husband's personhood and leadership involve? First, the wife's love of respect for her husband's personhood comprises of his intellect (mind), emotions (feelings) and volition (will or decision abilities):

1. The wife, by her love motivation and need-vow responsibility of marriage, is required to respect her husband's intellectual opinions, suggestions, and advice. If the wife disregards her husband's intellectual inputs by disregarding them and doing things her way, it is the undermining or disrespecting of his mental personhood abilities. If the wife keeps disregarding her husband's intellectual or mental

inputs in the marriage, she has rendered him incapable of using his mind. In other words, she is telling the husband that he has nothing intelligent to offer and that is why she does not regard his opinions, suggestions, and advice. A wife's attitude of disrespect of her husband's mental abilities and wisdom makes him begin to feel less of man and gradually renders him ineffective in the marriage.

2. The wife, by her love motivation and need-vow responsibility of marriage, is required to respect her husband's emotions. The wife by the motivation of her love-need vow responsibility must always remember to respect her husband's emotions by being careful not to do, show or say things which arouses negative emotions or feelings of disrespect.

One of the best ways the wife can make her husband powerful to do powerful things for her is to make him feel that he is special, the best and above reproach or disrespect. Arousing positive feelings of respect in your husband makes him stronger, effective, and more responsible. The reason is that his psyche shall begin to impress on him that much is given to him by his wife and therefore, much is required of him as affirmed in the Scriptures...*For everyone to whom much is given, from him much will be required; and to whom much has been committed, of him they will ask the more* **(Luke 12:48)**.

3. The wife, by her love motivation and need-vow responsibility of marriage, is required to respect her husband's volitional abilities to make right decisions or join her make right decision for their lives and marriage. In other words, wives should not forget to accord their husbands the due love respect of consulting and agreeing with their husbands before finalizing on any plans and decisions. By the same token, the husband as the servant leader of his home, cannot also do things without consulting and agreeing with his wife.

Second, the wife by her marital love-need vow responsibility is required to express the love-need of respect toward her husband's leadership as required by God's principles of marriage: *For the husband is head of the wife, as also Christ is head of the church; and He is the Savior of the body* (**Ephesians 5:23**). The headship or leadership of the husband over his family has nothing to do with him being the boss but rather, it requires him to be the servant, the responsible, the accountable, the provider and the protector of his wife and children. In the same way, Christ is although God and the head of His church…*but made Himself of no reputation, taking the form of a bondservant, and coming in the likeness of men* (**Philippians 2:7**) to redeem humanity through his sacrificial death.

The wife's respect of her husband's leadership empowers him to assume his full responsibility and accountability as the servant leader in their marital home. If the wife empowers her husband to lead his family, she will enjoy a loving, responsible, accountable, and efficient husband, and a servant leader. I have personally heard some wives accusing their husbands for not being responsible and being the kind of husbands, they ought to be. The problem here is partly from those husbands and partly from their wives.

To some extent, part of such irresponsibility can be traced back to the wives who refuse to allow and empower their husbands to be responsible by leading while leading alongside them. The other part of the problem is also from those husbands who need real help because their weaknesses are always out-weighing them and rendering them irresponsible.

Furthermore, what sometimes happen in certain marriages is that some wives render their own husbands irresponsible. They do that by pushing their husbands behind them to pave the way for them to take charge of the marriage and control the affairs of the home without the inputs of their husbands. God by His infinite wisdom took the wife from Adam's own side to emphasize the need to keep her always on his side of leadership **(Genesis 2:21-23)**. The intended purpose of God to position the wife on the very side of her husband was to avoid leadership intimidation and confusion in the marriage.

Hence, the wife's position in the life of her husband is clear and must not cause any confusion in the marriage. Therefore, the wife should not violate this fundamental principle of marriage to push the husband behind her. If the wife pushes her husband behind her, she has undermined his servant leadership to render him irresponsible and ineffective. In such situations, the husband's innate motivation to assume his full responsibility as servant leader gets demotivated.

Again, on average by default, a wife's disrespect of her husband's servant leadership, places him in a spectator position. If a husband remains in a spectator position for a long period, it will render him irresponsible, and make him dependent on his wife like a child. When God created man to bear the role of a husband, He obligated him to serve and give himself wholly to his wife and family as a servant and accountable leader.

God intentionally created the man first and gave him all the rules of the garden and was then charged to orient his wife with the same rules after she was brought to him as his wife. By doing so, he was assuming his servant leadership responsibility and accountability to his wife. The husband is not only the first responsible and accountable to his wife but also to God. In fact, that was the main reason why Adam could not understand why he was held as the first responsible and accountable one for violating the rule of eating from the forbidden tree. Adam became angry and disappointed and instead of accepting blame as a leader, he rather shifted blame to his wife.

Permit me to guess that Adam may have wondered why his wife did not show him the courtesy of discussing it with him before eating from the forbidden tree, if he was indeed the servant leader of their home? However, whatever he was thinking was not relevant because God had made him to be the first responsible and the accountable leader. Therefore, what Adam supposed to have done was to accept his irresponsibility as the leader of his home. But instead, he accused God of given him a wife who will not listen to him but rather preferred to do things her way. What Adam on his part forgot about was that his own negligence of meeting his wife's crying need of affection may have probably open the door for the intruder of their troubles.

The husband's servant leadership responsibility has a spiritual connotation. The fact is that it was Eve, Adam's wife who first ate from the tree of the knowledge of good and evil and yet he was and is still considered as responsible for the fall of mankind as stated: *Wherefore, as **by one man** sin entered into the world, and death by sin; and so, death passed upon all men, for that all have sinned* (**Romans 5:12**): It again parallels Adams leadership irresponsibility to Jesus' perfect leadership responsibility example as stated: *For if by one man's offence death reigned by one; much more they which receive abundance of grace and of the gift of righteousness shall reign in life by **one, Jesus Christ**.* (**Romans 5:17**).

Hence, by the same leadership principle of responsibility and accountability, Adam was made responsible for the fall of humanity. However, the righteousness of one-man, Jesus Christ and his sacrificial death has made available eternal to all those who repents and believe in Him as Lord and Savior. In effect, the Lord and Savior Jesus Christ has become the responsible head and the groom for His bride the church, which is the called-out saints and the faithful believers of God. To this end, wives are required by their own marital love-need vow responsibilities to submit to their own husbands through their love of respect of their husbands' personhood and leadership. By doing so intentionally, wives are able to help their husbands to become the husbands God intended them to be and the husband their wives expect them to be.

CHAPTER THREE

THE EXCLUSIVE RECIPROCAL OBLIGATORY LOVE OF ROMANCE

Spouses are required by their own love-need vow responsibilities to express their Exclusive Reciprocal Obligatory Love (EROL) of Romance to each other intentionally. The love of romance deals with specific and special love actions of gestures, pampering, utterances, touches, embraces, kisses, giving, services, and attention which are intended, or goal directed to arouse specific strong feelings of excitement, endearment, attachment, care, vulnerability, attraction of irresistibility, admiration, and pleasure. The romantic love actions are expressed through the five heart door senses of sight, smell, taste, hearing, and touch among lovers.

If spouses really desire to enjoy the love of romance, they have to make every intentional effort to unlock the doors of sweet love of romance which gets generated out of the heart. The activation key of romance is located inside of the heart. Loving spouses can only activate the bliss of romance by accessing all the five doors of the heart. The five doors of the heart can be accessed by fulfilling all the love-needs of the bodily five senses of sight, smell, taste, hearing, and touch in order to have each other's presence in the heart of endearment of each other as affirmed: *The **purposes of a person's heart are deep waters**, but **one who has insight draws them out*** (**Proverbs 20:5 NIV**).

The spouses who truly understand the importance of romance in marriage shall always commit to make every necessary effort to have their presence in the heart of each other. The place every spouse needs to be in the life of their spouse is in the heart in order to enjoy the best that is in each other. As already mentioned above, the spouses should do well to activate the strong and good love feelings of romantic excitement, endearment, attachment, care, vulnerability, attraction or irresistibility, admiration, and pleasure.

The EROL of romance is exclusive, reciprocal, and obligatory in marriage. Thus, the spouses must commit to express it mutually and enjoy it exclusively in order to maintain it in their marriage. The expression of marital romance is obligatory because it is one of the major life-lines of successful marriages and happy spouses. As a result, spouses should make it their lifestyle commitment to fulfill their love-need vow of romance to each other.

The question then is, how can spouses nurture the sweet love of romance in their marriages? First, spouses must commit to establish the royal principle of reciprocity as the foundation of their romantic love as stated: *If you really fulfill the* **royal law** *according to the Scripture, "You shall love your neighbor as yourself," you do well* **(James 2:8);** *"Therefore, whatever you want men to do to you, do also to them, for this is the Law and the Prophets* **(Matthew 7:12);** and *...Let each of you look out not only for his own interests, but also for the interests of others* **(Philippians 2:4).**

Second, the spouses must express the love of romance to each other intentionally through specific and special love actions of gestures, pampering, utterances, touches, embraces, kisses, giving, services, and attention. In doing so intentionally, the spouses will be able to arouse specific strong feelings of excitement, care, vulnerability, endearment, beauty, belonging, attachment, admiration, erotic pleasure, security, and the attraction of irresistibility.

Third, the spouses must commit to obtain romantic access into the heart through the five door senses to the loving heart of endearment as outlined below:

1. Romantic love can be discovered, nurtured, and expressed by asking questions to figure out what your spouse loves to see physically on, in and around you. After discovering those romantic desires of the eyes of each other, the spouses must then commit to satisfy them continuously, creatively and in style for establishing presence in each other's heart.

2. Romantic love can be discovered, nurtured, and expressed by asking questions to figure out what your spouse loves to smell on, in, and around you. The discovery of these romantic desires of the sense of smell of each other, must follow its commitment to satisfy those desires creatively and in style in order to have presence in each other's heart.

3. Romantic love can be discovered, nurtured, and expressed by asking questions to figure out what your spouse loves to taste. Again, the discovery of this romantic desire of the sense of taste of each other, must follow its commitment to satisfy those desires creatively and in style in order to have presence in each other's heart.

4. Romantic love can be discovered, nurtured, and expressed by asking questions to figure out what your spouse loves to hear. Discovering what your spouse loves to hear is extremely important in romantic marriages. Spouses must never forget that both positive and negative utterances have both lasting positive and negative impacts on the lives of romantic spouses. Exploring and figuring out what your spouse loves to hear from you is the pathway to fulfilling romantic love-needs. The discovery of the romantic pathways must then lead to intentional and continuous fulfillment of those romantic hearing love-needs in a creative, sweet, comforting, arous-

ing, and wooing style in order to have presence in each other's heart.

5. Romantic love can be discovered, nurtured, and expressed by asking questions and exploring on each other to figure out how your spouse loves to be touched, kissed, fondled, embraced, and engage in sexual intercourse. Discovery must lead to continuous learning of each other's bodies, which must also lead to all possible efforts to satisfy the love-need sense of touch on your spouse creatively and in style. Fulfilling the love-needs of romance to your spouse intentionally and continuously, allow the spouses to have a permanent presence in the heart of each other.

Hence, spouses should never forget to express romantic love because both spouses feed on it for their emotional nourishment and mental soundness.

CHAPTER FOUR

EXCLUSIVE RECIPROCAL OBLIGATORY LOVE OF INTIMACY

The Exclusive Reciprocal Obligatory Love (EROL) of Intimacy in marriage is the process of developing a complete knowledge and trust for each other as spouses. The complete knowledge and trust of intimacy is resulted from vulnerability, honesty, nakedness, transparency, closeness, shamelessness, shylessness, sexual fulfillment and commonness in everything among spouses. Hence, love of intimacy in marriage is about mutual deepest knowledge and trust which comes through predictability, close attachment, sexual bonding and full access to each other's mind and emotions by becoming completely available and vulnerable to each other without fear, shame, and shy as affirmed: *And **they were both naked**, the **man and his wife**, and **were not ashamed*** **(Genesis 2:25).**

Spouses should always remember that first, the marital love-need of intimacy is exclusive to the spouses only because the sharing of it with any other person outside the marriage is a betrayal of trust and the dismantling of marriage bond. Second, the marital love-need of intimacy is reciprocal, in the sense that it cannot be truly fulfilled one-sidedly by a spouse. Rather, it supposed to be mutually fulfilled to each spouse willing and lovingly. Third, the marital love-need of intimacy is obligatory because it is a critical to the happiness of the spouses and success of the marriage. Hence, the spouses should not neglect their own love-need vow responsibility to fulfill intimacy to each other by ensuring and having each other's trust, happiness, pleasure, bonding, and security.

The Exclusive Reciprocal Obligatory Love of intimacy is neither automatic nor instant. Rather, it is a process in marriage whereby, spouses intentionally and lovingly commit to cleave the six important elements of their lives to ensure complete intimacy. The complete marital intimacy results from the intentional love commitment to cleave or stick together their intellects (minds), emotions (feelings), volitions (will power of decision), conscience (moral awareness of right and wrongs), intuitions (center of ideas) and body of the souses.

The Bible recommends cleaving as the process for building the genuine exclusive reciprocal obligatory love of intimacy as stated: *Therefore, shall a man leave his father and his mother, and shall **cleave** unto his wife: and they shall be **one flesh**.* **(Genesis 2:24 KJV).** Cleaving simply means sticking together. The questing to ask in order to determine the process of intimacy is this; what is the process by which spouses can cleave in order to enjoy intimacy? First, they have to stick together what is inside their heart. Second, they have to stick together their bodies. The are six areas in the life of the spouses which they must intentionally commit to initiate the cleaving process of intimacy are as follows:

1. **Intimacy through the Spouses' Intellects** - Spouses by the motivation of their own love-need vows must commit to cleave their intellects into one to enhance intimacy. The cleaving process of intimacy in marriage is made possible by allowing full access into each other's mind of thoughts, perceptions, expectations, plans, likes and dislikes. The complete access into each spouse's mind requires openness and honest communication about everything in each other's life. Failure to communicate openly and honestly destroys trust in marriage. The love-need vow responsibilities of marriage, require the spouses to give each other the full right to know each other closely or intimately. The result of a complete mental intimacy is predictability of each other as honest and close spouses.

2. **Intimacy through the Spouses' Emotions** - Spouses by the motivation of their own love-need vows must commit to cleave their emotions into one by being transparent with each other's feelings. The spouses' readiness to share both positive and negative feelings without harboring them is the

pathway to their emotional intimacy and health. The best way for spouses to cleave their emotions is by consciously avoiding the arousal of negative feelings of displeasure, disrespect, dishonor, condescension, bitterness, fear, jealousy, and anger. Spouse's must be ready to share their negative emotions, most especially in situations when the offender spouse has not realized his or her fault. The humble and loving thing to do when prompted by your spouse with regards to wrongs is to quickly admit and apologize to settle disagreement or conflict amicably.

3. **Intimacy through the Spouses' Volitions** - Spouses by the motivation of their own love-need vow must commit to cleave their volitions into one to effect intimacy in their marriage. The intimacy through cleaving of volitions of the spouses is made possible by committing to involve each other in all plans and decisions of individual life and the marriage. Spouses must involve each other in the exercise of their volitional powers by discussing and agreeing on decisions before execution. Interestingly, marriage does not only bond two bodies into one, but it also merges their soul and spirit into oneness of full intimacy. Spouses must, therefore, realize that marital decisional responsibility is a mutual one. Hence, spouses should be careful not to manipulate each other by claiming the decisional powers in the marriage because it is a violation of the law of marital intimacy.

4. **Intimacy through the Spouses' Consciences** - Spouses by the motivation of their own love-need vow must commit to cleave their conscience into one to allow intimacy to flourish in their marriage. The conscience is the center of innate awareness of morality. The innate morality awareness of right and wrongs has two-way effects: The right actions affirm inner peace, and the wrong actions disturb the inner peace of the spouses as affirmed: *They show that the essential requirements of the **Law are written in their hearts;** and **their conscience** [their sense of right and wrong, their moral choices] **bearing witness** and their **thoughts alternately accusing or perhaps defending them*** (**Romans 2:15, AMP**).

   The spouses are therefore, required by their own love-need vows to be conscious of their own wrongs, admit them, and quickly make amends. Amends of marital faults are made possible through a quick mutual submission of admission, apology, and forgiveness to clear the path for intimate cleaving as affirmed: *Love prospers when a fault is forgiven but dwelling on it separates close friends* (**Proverbs 17:9 NLT**).

5. **Intimacy through the Spouses' Intuitions** - Spouses by the motivation of their own love-need vows must commit to cleave their intuitions into one to allow intimacy to develop in their marriage. The cleaving of intuition requires mutual sharing,

owning, and enjoying the benefits of individual ideas for greater achievements and results. Intimate cleaving of intuitive ideas should not be limited to just sharing and owning but also utilizing each other's ideas, knowledge, and expertise to achieve greater goals in the marriage for mutual enjoyment.

6. **Intimacy through the Spouses' Bodies** - Spouses by the motivation of their own love-need vows must commit to cleave their bodies into one to allow intimacy to develop in their marriage. Marital bodily intimacy is made possible through the voluntary exchange of the rights each other wields over his or her own body. The ultimate way by which the two bodies can reach oneness bonding is through the spouses' commitment to satisfactorily meet each other's sexual needs willingly, intentionally, and selflessly. The free-flowing, and intentional satisfaction of each other's sexual needs of ecstasy is the express way of bodily intimacy. Spouses must, therefore, see to satisfy each other's sexual needs by initiating and receiving sex freely in order to reinforce bodily bonding of oneness.

Intimacy through bodily cleaving, bolsters confidence in each other in the process where each spouse is freely allowed to express their sexual needs by admiring each other's body. In ensuring intimacy of bodily cleaving, the spouses must be careful not to undermine each other by using any bodily blemishes to castigate or make fun of each other. Such unloving, demeaning, and shameful behavior generates low self-esteem issues in each other to destroy intimacy and happiness in marriage. If a spouse cares to correct or comment on negative thing physically, it shall be best to help correct it empathetically than to comment on it to create undermining feelings. In caring for each other, spouses must always remember to apply the principle of human dignity of respect, self-worth, and self-protectiveness.

Furthermore, intentional affirmation and admiration of each other's body of beauty, and self-worth generate high attraction among spouses. The unhindered marital intimacy through the cleaving of the two hearts and bodies removes shyness, shame, fear, and low self-esteem. Intimacy in this high level allows self-confidence and exciting sexual expressions to thrive in the marriage.

7. **Intimacy through Marital All-in-Commonness -** Spouses by the motivation of their own love-need vows must commit to cleave by having all things in common for mutual benefit. Hence, the exclusive reciprocal obligatory love of intimacy should motivate the spouses to commit to mutually own and benefit from everything in their lives. Intimacy by principle, requires the spouses to fully cleave all things in, of, and around them, for mutual ownership and enjoyment in the marriage. The spouses should also commit to develop intentional intimacy and liking for each other's hobbies to some accommodative extent.

PART 5

THE NEED-VOW PURPOSE OF MARRIAGE

CHAPTER ONE

INDISPENSABLE LOVE-NEED PURPOSE OF MARRIAGE

The central purpose of marriage is about meeting specific and indispensable needs of life. It was God who instituted marriage and intended it to meet both specific and indispensable needs of life. Marriage, in fact, fulfills one of the very core divine purposes for mankind with regards their relationship and life progress. Consequently, the marital needs fulfillment purpose forms the core basis for all the other purposes of marriage. Marriage by God design has several purposes. However, every spouse must not forget that the very core or the foundational purpose among them all is the need-fulfillment responsibilities among spouses.

God in His infinite wisdom created Adam and his wife with innate needs which require the commitment from each other to fulfill them lovingly and intentionally. In other words, God has endowed both the husband and the wife with the ability to satisfy each other's mental, emotional, volitional, and physical needs. The Bible describes the marital needs fulfillment with these words: *And the LORD God said, "It is not good that man should be alone; I will make him a helper comparable to him* (**Genesis 2:18**)." In the garden was found so many different kinds of animals; however, none was comparable or suitable or had the innate capabilities to provide the partnership and the fulfilling support Adam needed as also affirmed: *So, Adam gave names to all cattle, to the birds of the air, and to every beast of the field. But for Adam there was not found a helper comparable to him* (**Genesis 2:20**).

It was God who instituted the comparable or suitable partnership principle of marriage, and yet, He did not consider Himself as the right person to satisfy such an important need of marital couple. The reason is that a spirit and mortal cannot equally share and have all things in common. Even for God to accomplish the purpose of redemption, He could not even do it in any other way except through the incarnation of Jesus by the natural course of life.

The Man and the woman were designed by God and were made fully capable to provide each other's need to fulfill their own happiness and achieve the best for their lives. Eve, as noted above, was brought into the marriage by God to assume the full responsibility to become the suitable wife to provide the suitable help Adam needed in order to be happy and fulfilled. By the same vein, Adam also received Eve as wife to assume his full responsibility of becoming the suitable husband to provide the support she needed in order to be happy and fulfilled.

Interestingly, Adam assumed his full responsibility to fulfill his wife's needs as his very own. Adam in declaring his love commitment to meet his wife's needs, he affirmed to treat her as the bone of his very bones and the flesh of his very flesh **(Genesis 2:23).** In the same manner, the wife was expected to fulfil her husband's needs by treating him as the bone of her very bones and flesh of her very flesh.

The reason for the marital need-fulfillment dynamics is that the marital need is reciprocal by the principle of giving and receiving. Humans by nature love and care for themselves. However, spouses are required by their love-need vow responsibilities to extend their self-nurtured love and care to each other as affirmed in the Scriptures: *For no one ever **hated his own flesh**, but **nourishes** and **cherishes** it, just as the Lord does the church* **(Ephesians 5:29);** ***Owe no one anything except to love one another***, *for he who loves another has fulfilled the law* **(Romans 13:8).**

Any aspirant of marriage must come to the ultimate understanding that the onset failure of marriage is to marry and remain selfish and self-centered. Selfishness and self-centeredness in marriage cause spouses to refuse to pay their love debt to each other. When spouses continue to neglect the payment of their love debt to each other, they shall continue to drop their love credit scores to start causing a great deal of displeasure in marriage. When spouses continue to neglect the payment of their love debt to each other for an extended period of time, they will end up losing their marital love creditworthiness. Love-credit unworthiness in marriage is the foundational cause of marital displeasures, and heartbreaks in all suffering and unhappy marriages around the world.

Interestingly enough, God created everything in this universe to need each other for effective operations. The universe needs its elements to operate consistently and constantly to ensure its regular and effective functioning. In the same way, God designed all the parts of and within the body to depend on each other for effective operation and functioning. The moment one part becomes less effective, the other parts begin to suffer. So is marriage, if the spouses refuse to fulfill each other's love-needs, the marriage shall surely become dysfunctional to affect both spouses adversely.

Adam's agreement to marry Eve signified his full assumption of his love-need vow responsibility to meet and care for his wife's love-needs, just as he commits to meet his own needs. In the same manner, Eve's, agreement to marry Adam also signified her full assumption of her love-need vow responsibility to meet her husband's specific love-needs, just as she fulfills her own needs. Therefore, when a man and a woman marry, they have vowed to obligate themselves to commit willingly and intentionally to meet each other's love-needs for lifetime.

CHAPTER TWO

MEANING OF VOW WITH ITS IMPLICATIONS IN MARRIAGE

A vow is a sacred, solemn, and voluntary pledge of commitment to undertake a personal or agreed list of things. First, the sacredness of a vow emphasizes its required respect and honor; and so, spouses are cautioned against the treatment of their vows with contempt and dishonor. Second, the solemness of a vow also emphasizes seriousness and sincerity; and so, spouses are cautioned against the treatment of their vows with unseriousness and unfaithfulness. Couples are therefore, required to be serious minded in approaching marriage because its vows are sacred and solemn, requiring voluntary commitment to fulfill its love-needs in marriage for lifetime.

Marriage by God's order obligates the spouses into a voluntary and mutual vow to fulfill each other's love-needs in order to ensure the success of their marriage. Hence, when a man and a woman agree to marry and initiate the marriage, both spouses have pledged their sacred and solemn commitment to fulfill each other's love-need vow responsibilities to each other for lifetime. When spouses consciously and lovingly assume their full love-need vow responsibilities to each other, it shall generate high attraction among each other as spouses.

The marital love-need vow responsibilities require reciprocal or mutual correspondent responses; and therefore, cannot be fulfilled one-sidedly. The reason being that marital love-need vows require the fulfillment of each spouse's respective responsibilities to each other in order to create balance of love and happiness in the marriage. The surprising thing about the marital love-need vow is that if the spouses refuse to fulfill their own vow responsibilities to each other, the happiness of both spouses shall be compromised. This is because the principle of sowing and reaping affirms that a person only reaps what have been sown and what have not been sown leaves nothing to be reaped. If a person should reap what he or she has not sown, that will be considered stealing, which comes with both self-inflicting and general consequences.

Again, if both spouses would understand the sacredness and the solemnness of their vows and commit to fulfill its required responsibilities by the motivation of their love, both spouses cannot but cherish themselves and become irresistible to each other. When these love-need vow responsibilities are intentionally and cheerfully rendered between spouses, they have assured themselves of marital success and happiness without regret. The neglect of the spouses' own vows to meet each other's love-needs, being motivated by selfishness and self-centeredness, have always been the cause of marital disappointments and heartbreaks, with its subsequent fallouts. In the following final part, I will be dealing with ten specific love-need vow responsibilities of marriage.

PART SIX

TEN NEED-VOW RESPONSIBILITIES OF MARRIAGE

CHAPTER ONE

VOW TO LEAVE BEHIND ALL INTRUSIONS AGAINST YOUR MARRIAGE FOR LIFETIME

*Therefore, a man **shall leave** his **father and mother** and be joined to his wife, and they shall become one flesh* **(Genesis 2:24).**

One of the initial vow requirements of marriage is the aspect of leaving behind each other all intrusions against the marriage. Intrusion in marriage deals with the unauthorized control and interruptions that always seek to influence the spouses and their choices or decisions in the marriage. The spouses by the motivation of their love-need vows are required to leave behind all marital intrusions of control, interruptions, and infringements which serve as impediments to their own happiness and the success of the marriage. God from the very onset of marriage required every couple to leave behind themselves known intrusive threats to their marriage as expressed in the following verse of Scripture: *Therefore, a man shall* **leave his father and mother** *and* **be joined to his wife**, *and they shall become* **one flesh**.

As the man commits to observe his leave-behind vow requirements, the woman must also follow suit to observe her part of the same vow to create the happiness and the peace balance both expect in their marriage. The leave-behind principle of marriage is a vice versa principle and as a result, it cannot be done one-sidedly among spouses. When marital leaving is done by just one spouse, the marriage shall begin to suffer in the course of time. The life of marriage as was intended by God is supposed to be mutually controlled and managed by only the husband and his wife with the commitment to meet each other's needs. Marital intrusive influences are like deadly virus. It has the propensity to fight the health of marriages, and gradually leads them to the grave with much confusion and heartbreaks.

Life is full of negative influences and influencers who try to control and undermine the purposes, affairs, and decisions of peoples' lives. Spouses are therefore, required to be aware and be ready to resist all negative influences and influencers against their own happiness and marital success without compromise. Marital intrusion is dangerous to every marriage in the sense that it always seeks to gain unauthorized access to control and interrupt the affairs of marriages from its right course and purpose.

Spouses must never forget that all intrusive forces are required to remain outside their marriage. The good news is that no intrusion has the power to enter into the marriage without the authorization of the spouses. Hence, the failure to resist marital intrusion is an indirect way of impeding the success of one's own marriage. The most dangerous mistake Mrs. Eve Adam made which brought serious confusion to her marriage was the permission she gave to Satan, by which he utilized to misguide the course of their lives and marriage. Satan's permitted intrusion in the marriage of Mr. & Mrs. Adam led to the stifling of their own happiness and the success of their general lives.

Marriage, therefore, requires wisdom, and intentional commitment to resist all intrusive influences and influencers which are always seeking to change the right course of marriages. The life of every marriage should be mutually managed and controlled by the spouses alone. Once again, let me reiterate that marital intrusive influences are like a deadly virus which has the propensity to fight the health of marriages, and gradually leads it to the grave with much confusion and heartbreaks. As a result, any spouse who truly desires to enjoy marriage should be ready and committed to say goodbye to the following seven major potential intrusive influences which may seek to fight the success and the health of marital relationships:

1. Vow to Leave the Intrusions of Ego for Lifetime

Marriage by divine order and principles requires both spouses to commit to their love-need vow responsibilities to leave behind the negative intrusions of ego. The word "ego" originates from Latin, meaning "I" or "self." Interestingly, Greek has a similar word which is transliterated as "philautia" meaning "love of self." In this context, I will explore ego and parallel it with "philautia" in the sense of love of self.

Ego and philautia have both positive and negative or healthy and unhealthy orientations. The positive ego of the love of self, comprises of self-esteem, self-respect, self-admiration and self-worth or importance. However, the negative ego of self-love manifests in self-conceit or selfishness, self-centeredness, self-indulgence, self-glory, superiority, arrogance, and greed.

Naturally...*no one ever **hated his own flesh**, but **nourishes** and **cherishes it**, just as the Lord does the church* (**Ephesians 5:29**). The Lord Jesus nourishes and cherishes the church because it is His bride and own body. As we know, the Lord Jesus paid the eternal death of sin's penalty of humanity with His life through the humiliations, abuses, sufferings, and the ultimate brutal death he experienced on the cross. However, He resurrected and declared victory over sin and Satan on behalf of His church, the redeemed. In the same vein, the spouses by their love-need vows of marriage are required to cherish and nourish each other's body and life in any way possible as follows:

First, the love-need vow of marriage with regards to the healthy love of self, requires all spouses to intentionally commit to offer to their loving spouses their very best of life. In other words, the same or more self-care of cherishment, nourishment and endearment developed and desired for self must be giving to each other in the marriage to affirm the mutual marital love as affirmed: *Therefore, what-*

ever you want men to do to you, do also to them, for this is the Law and the Prophets **(Matthew 7:12).** Healthy self-love always develops the following virtue which must in turn impact each other in the other positively:

1. **Healthy Self-love of Self-esteem** - Healthy love of self, nurtures into self-esteem which the marital love-need vow obligates the spouses to treat each other likewise.

2. **Healthy Self-love of Self-respect** - Healthy self-love develops into self-respect which should motivate the spouses to accord each other the same respect and even more.

3. **Healthy Self-love of Self-admiration** - Healthy love of self develops into self-admiration of good self-perception of beauty, wonder, pleasure, and approval which must also obligate each spouse to accord the same or more to each other.

4. **Healthy Self-love of Self-worth** - Healthy love of self develops a person's self-worth or self-importance by which spouses are also required by their own vows to promote each other's self-worth.

5. **Healthy Self-love of Self-care** - Healthy love of self, is motivated to care for one's own emotions and also cherish and nourish one's own body. Spouses by the motivation of their love-need vows are required to do the same or more for each other.

Second, however, the love-need vow responsibilities of marriage require all spouses to commit to leave behind the marriage their own unhealthy love of self. Consequently, the refusal to leave behind each other's unhealthy self-love is bound to jeopardize the success of the marriage and toxify its health. Unhealthy love of self is the excessive self-love devoid of concern for other's enjoyment of respect, cherishment, care, nourishment, endearment, and protection as clearly stated: *Let nothing be done through* ***selfish ambition or conceit****, but in* ***lowliness of mind*** *let each* ***esteem others better than himself****. 4 Let each of you look out* ***not only for his own_interests, but also for the interests of others*** (Philippians 2:3).

Unhealthy self-love manifests itself in at least six ways. If spouses, however, contract marriage without leaving their unhealthy self-love behind, right from the word go, they have preset their marriage for failure, confusion, hurt, and heartbreaks as follows:

1. **Unhealthy Self-love of Selfishness** - The unhealthy self-love manifests itself in self-conceit or selfishness which in a sense concentrates all concern and care for one's own needs, interests, pleasures, and wellbeing. The unhealthy love of self is always motivated by selfishness which neglects each spouses' love-needs of interests, respect, cherishment, care, nourishment, endearment, and protection.

2. **Unhealthy Self-love of Self-centeredness** - The unhealthy self-love of self-centeredness causes a spouse to think and care only about self. The

continuous nurturing of self-love of self-centeredness after marriage shall result in a spouse to think, care, regard and serve one's own interests and benefits to the neglect of one's own spouse's needs and interests. Self-centeredness generates attitudes such as: "I don't feel like doing this or that"; "I need my privacy"; "I want to be alone"; "I do not want to be bothered"; "I am not in the mood"; "I need a space"; "I have to be right or I am always right"; "I don't say sorry" or "I hate to say sorry"; "I am used to this or that"; "I am not used to this or that", and many such self-preoccupying attitude phrases. If a couple carry their egocentric baggage into their marriage, the marital happiness and success are compromised and as a result, they should not expect to enjoy happiness in their marriage.

3. **Unhealthy Self-love of Self-indulgence** - The unhealthy self-love of self-indulgence excessively seeks and does whatever satisfies one's own lust without consideration for other people's feelings. Self-indulgence has influenced so many spouses to betray their own trust and had violated their love-need vow of respect and faithfulness to each other. Self-indulgent spouses despise their own marriage love-need vows to wrongfully satisfy their lust of the eye, flesh, and pride of their life **(1John.2:16).**

By the uncontrolled lust of the eyes, some spouses have gone their way by flirting with others who are not their spouses. Others, by their insatiable lust of both eye and flesh have been led to pornographic addiction or infidelities or both. Furthermore, the uncontrolled lust of the flesh has also led many spouses to infidelities, alcoholism, and drug abuses which have generated into irresolvable conflicts in so many marriages and homes. Again, by the lust of the pride of life, many have been led to the road of the condescending evil of comparison of beauty, fame, wealth, education, and status which has led to the destruction of so many marriages.

4. **Unhealthy Self-love of Self-glory** - The unhealthy self-love of self-glory or vainglory has led many spouses to exaggerate their own self-worth, beauty, knowledge, expertise, capabilities and achievements to the demeaning and neglect of their spouse' love-needs by causing a lot of hurts, disappointments, and heartbreaks.

5. **Unhealthy Self-love of Greed** - The marital unhealthy self-love of greed has also influenced so many spouses to use both personal and joint resources for secret personal benefits to the total neglect of the needs of the other spouse and the marriage.

6. **Unhealthy Self-love of Superiority** - The marital unhealthy self-love of superiority is a self-claim ego of being superior, greater, honorable, better, important, and smarter to the demeaning of one's own spouse.

The unhealthy evils of ego against the purpose of marriage are daunting and so detrimental to the health, and success of every marriage. The caution therefore is this: Marital couples must not forget to leave behind them their unhealthy ego before declaring intentions to marry. The fact still remains that every serious-minded candidate of marriage should make every effort and a continuous commitment to fulfill their love-need vow to leave behind their lives, the negative intrusions of both ego and philautia of self-love.

2. Vow to Leave the Intrusions of Parents for Lifetime

Marriage by divine order requires both parents to release and support their mature sons and daughters into marriage without further interruption, usurping of authority and control after their marriage. Both the man and the woman who decide to marry are also required by God and their own love-need vows to leave father and mother in order to allow the cleaving of the two heterosexual couple to grow their oneness in everything **(Genesis 2:24)** for their lifetime.

Leaving behind parents has to do with leaving behind their intrusive influences to give way for the new spouses to live and make responsible decisions for their own lives. Responsible and loving parents should do well not to interrupt and exert their control over their children's marriage. God's order of marriage requires parent to support their adult children to marry and also commit to hand over their lives' authority to them as a proof of their adulthood with its responsibilities. The marriage which is free from parental intrusion of control enables the new spouses to develop their marital maturity to ensure the success of their own marriage.

The spouses on the other hand, must also develop the willingness to leave behind the unauthorized influences and control of each other's parents. The spouses' willingness and commitment to leave behind their parental control enable them to harness their own authority and control over their own lives and the lives of their future children. Naturally by average, most parents love their children, and they are even required by their parental responsibilities to teach their children the right ways of life **(Proverbs 22:6).** There are some parents, who find it so difficult to let go their children after their marriage. Despite the fact of releasing their children into marriage, they still seek every avenue to impress their inputs on their marital decisions.

Moreover, there are some spouses on the other hand, who are so inclined to their parents to the extent that there is nothing they can comfortably do in their marriage without soliciting for their parents' inputs. Please, do not get me wrong, for there is nothing wrong with seeking advice from parents on certain issues. However, if it becomes a routine, parental control shall become unbearably strong to affect the marriage in the course of time.

After marriage, the sons and daughters should be allowed to apply all the knowledge they have acquired from the teachings and coaching of their parents without interruptions. If parents try to always intrude into the marriage of their children without being consulted for their inputs, such external interruptions usually disengage the spouses from maturing by making mutual decisions and bearing its responsibilities.

Loving parents shall always be there for their children and their counsel shall always be available for them. However, there must always be the agreement between the spouses to solicit the advice of parents on specific issues they so choose. In all, it does not matter the advice received from parents, the decision must always be made by the spouses themselves mutually. The allowed intrusive influence, no matter where it is coming from, can be toxic and dangerous to the health of marriages.

3. Vow to Leave the Intrusion of Children for Lifetime

The one aspect of intrusion which can easily control spouses and interrupt their decisions without being easily realized is that of the intrusive manipulative influences of children. Psychological research has revealed that children even at their early stages can easily manipulate their parents to do things their way all the time without them realizing the negative effects of such actions. It can even get to a point where some parents can be so influenced to the extent that they become extremely prone to their own children to do what they wish and request.

The love of parents for their children to some extent has the propensity to make them vulnerable to the intrusive influences of their children. When spouses lose guard over the intrusions of their children, they shall end up pleasing the children to the neglect of their own decisions and pleasing each other as spouses for the benefit of the marital home. Spouses must understand that children are not supposed to be allowed to make decisions or control decisions of the marital home. The simple reason is that it is not their role and responsibility to make decisions for the family. It is the responsibility of parents to teach their children the right way of life so that they can mature to embrace it **(Proverbs 22:6).**

Under no circumstance should spouses allow their children to control their marital decisions which in the end will not be in the best interest of the children themselves. If parents become less conscious to agree on all matters with regards to their children, the children can easily manipulate one of the parents to side with their wants and misconducts, to even use that to escape discipline and even create conflicts between their parents.

Again, under no circumstance should spouses disagree with each other just to please their children with regards to wants and discipline. There have been instances whereby the spouses undermine each other's inputs just to submit to the dictates or pleasures of their children. There are also times when a spouse will listen to a concern of their child and instantly believe it without even asking the other spouse of their version as affirmed in Scripture: *The first one to plead his cause seems right, until his neighbor comes and examines him* **(Proverbs 18:17).** When spouses allow such manipulations, the children can easily lie against each other to cause trouble for the marriage and their home. Situations like this have caused a lot of continuous conflicts and the downfall of many marriages.

Spouses should, therefore, be very circumspect not to side with their children by disputing among themselves in the presence of the children. The spouses should also be careful not to tolerate their complaints against each other. Failure to safeguard themselves against such manipulations shall motivate them to even lie or slander against each other; most especially when they don't get their way with another parent. However, it is always good to search and know the truth in order to enable the reasonable resolution with your own spouse or the child.

In all these complications, the spouses are obligated by their own love-need vow responsibilities to first please themselves but love and care for the children. When spouses shift their loyalty and trust from each other to their children, they have made their marriage liable to confusion, conflicts, and heartbreaks. The spouses by divine requirement of parenthood are however, required to care, provide, protect, train, and coach their children in the right ways of life. When the children mature to rights and wrongs, they can be allowed to contribute ideas or suggestions, but they are not supposed to force it on the parents. Moreover, they should never be allowed to make demands and control decisions and affairs of the marital home.

4. Vow to Leave the Intrusive Influences of Siblings for Lifetime

Marriage by divine order obligates the spouses of their own love-need vow responsibilities not to give in to the intrusive influences of their siblings. Brothers and sisters shall always remain part of the family and each other may wield some form of influence in the life of each other's sibling. However, siblings should not be allowed to neither interrupt the affairs of the marriage nor wield any form of control to influence marital decisions.

Intrusions from siblings can be very dangerous and unhealthy to marital success and happiness of the spouses. Spouses must be conscious not to open such a door of intrusion, for it usually hurt marital loving relationships. By nature on average, humans by their ego of selfishness, self-centeredness, pride, superiority, and greed would always want to decide for others.

However, if spouses really want to enjoy their marriage and its success, they must be ready not to allow siblings to intrude their marriage, control and make decisions for them. It is laudable for siblings to submit their ideas to their siblings in a form of suggestions only. In fact, if there is a sibling who so desire to influence and control other people's marriage, it shall be best to exercise such control and concentrate all their influences over their own marriage and life to make them better and successful.

5. Vow to Leave the Intrusions of Friends for Lifetime

Marriage by its love-need vow responsibilities should remind the spouses to leave behind the intrusions of friends for the rest of their lives. Friendships and confidants of trust are always developed before a person meets their love potential partner for marriage. However, after marriage, those friends can no longer play the role of confidants with whom every life detail is freely shared. The confidant role of trust and total disclosure must be turned over to the spouses who have committed to become one in everything in marriage without shame, shy or fear.

Genuine friendship provides vital support to its friends and to some extent relate to each other as confidants who trust and share the deep things of life with each other. Again, friends to some extent influence each other's decisions of life. However, after marriage, such closeness and confidant trust of transparency and detail sharing should be between the spouses alone.

The friends of each other's spouse must be introduced to each other, but they should not be ever allowed to interrupt the affairs of the marriage and somehow wield any form of control over the decisions of their marriage. The spouses by agreement may seek the advice of their friends depending on their maturity and expertise but the decision must be theirs to make without any interruptions. It is always best to seek marital life impactful counsel from a marriage expert. It is required of the husband and the wife to make every effort to become each other's closest friend, confidant of trust, and adviser. When spouses trust, share, support and have all things in common in their marriage, success and happiness shall not just be a desire but shall be a reality.

6. Vow to Leave the Intrusions of Vocation for Lifetime

Marriage by its love-need vow responsibilities require the spouses to leave behind the intrusive influences of vocation for the rest of their lives. Vocation with regards to each other's job can at times intrude the marriage and interrupt its closeness and desired attention from each other. After marriage, each other's job should not control and wield the entire attention of the marriage. Despite the busy schedules, the spouses must devote time for themselves to bond through romantic care, conversations, outings, vacations, smooches, and satisfying sex. Spouses must never forget to engage in intentional anticipated dating to have fun, closeness, and arouse good romantic feelings.

Although, working to bring in money is an essential element of marital success and happiness. However, spouses must determine to spend time together to avoid marital aloneness which subsequently leads to loneliness. There have been instances where certain spouses give reason beyond doubt that they love their job more than their significant partner and the life of their marriage.

There are some individuals who are workaholics and are married to their jobs. However, if they really want to enjoy their marriage, there must be a divorce of the original spouse which is their job. In other words, the spouses must be motivated by love to efficiently manage their vocational schedule in order to dedicate attention for each other's love-needs. There should be a paradigm shift from being a workaholic to a loving spouse who admires, cares, and endears your spouse greatly.

Loving spouses must be careful not to neglect their love-need vow responsibility to resist any vocational intrusion of control and interruptions against their marital closeness, attention, and care. Surprisingly, marital jealousy extends to any person or thing which may try to vie the attention and love each spouse deserves. Loving spouses must be careful not to arouse unnecessary vocational intrusive jealousy, for such will not augur well for the success of the marriage and the happiness of each other.

7. Vow to Leave Intrusions of Social Media for Lifetime

Nowadays, the Social Networking Media such as Facebook, LinkedIn, Google Plus, Twitter, Tumblr, Instagram, Snapshot, Pinterest, YouTube, Periscope, Vimeo, and others have been an aggressive intrusion against marital closeness and attention. The internet on the other hand has made every information and diverse lifestyles readily available on our phones. As a result, the internet which has made the world a global village and has given instant access to every social media has made its intrusion extremely aggressive. The internet has in fact, been gaining great control and has steadily been gaining undue attention of the masses and many spouses to the neglect of the attention their loved ones deserve.

Unfortunately, many have been gripped into its deep temptations and have not been able to control its intrusions of the lust of the eyes, flesh, and pride of its deceitful life portrayals. As a result of the misusage and mismanagement of internet and social media, many spouses have even lost touch with each. Social media intrusion has been having so much adverse effect on marriages and have been vying the attention and closeness spouses deserve from each other.

Sadly enough, some spouses have become so much addicted to browsing everything on the internet and the social media to the extent that when they are even together, they are alone because they give most attention to their phones. Despite all the intrusions in our world which are vying for our attention, spouses must come to the full realization of their own marital love-need vows which require them to resist anything which tries to rob them of the attention and closeness each one deserves from each other.

In fact, it is selfish and self-centered to directly or indirectly portray to your own spouse that a particular form of social media or the browsing on the internet is worthy of your attention more than your spouse. So many marriages in our world today are growing cold day by day and many spouses are feeling more isolated and lonelier than ever. According to Darren Adamson, PhD, LMFT, and Chair of the Department of Marriage and Family Sciences at Northcentral University, there are three major potential dangers social media pose to marriages:

> [5]*First, social media serves as a distraction from focusing on the interactions that nurture relationships. Second, people share their best lives on social media, so couples sometimes compare their mundane lives with other's exciting lives, which can create destructive comparisons; And third, there is the potential for another relationship that looks so much better than the primary relationship.*

---

5. 2017, https://www.ncu.edu/blog/dangers-social-media-marriage-and-family#gref). Assessed 12 January 2021.

> *This can lead to extra-couple relationships that ultimately destroy the primary relationship...*

Despite the odds and evasive intrusions of the internet or the social media, spouses can rather utilize them to their advantage to enhance their communication while away from each other or even together. Spouses must as well see to resist its enticing control, interruptions, and distractions. If proper boundaries are not set to control the undue intrusive influences of the internet and the social media, spouses will end up robbing themselves of the attention, and closeness each deserves. When this happens, it will start draining out the health and life of the marriage which gradually shall lead to confusion, hurts, and heartbreaks. The spouses must, therefore, motivate themselves by their love-need vows to use the internet and the social media responsibly to enhance their marital relationship. The spouses, however, must spend time to nurture their love for each other than to give way for various life's intrusions to starve each other of the deserved closeness and attention from each other.

CHAPTER TWO

VOW TO LOVE EACH OTHER WITH THE SEVEN MULTIFUNCTIONAL APPLIED LOVE FOR LIFETIME

Marriage by its love-need vows require the spouses to also express the seven multifunctional applied love (MAL) to each other for a lifetime. Since love is pivotal to successful and well-functioning marriages, it must be better understood, and its principles and responsibilities rightly applied. Love is extremely popular, but it is the most misused word by both old and young. Many references love to insignificant things like ice-cream, chocolate, games, and many other such trifles, which have actually reduced the significance of love to only feelings and infatuations. When a foundational meaning of a subject is not properly established, it leads to misunderstanding, misuse, and misapplication. The same can be said about love. However, for marriage to be both successful and enjoyable, its foundation needs to be constructed right as already emphasized in the early parts of this book.

Furthermore, as already referenced, love is the willingness, the commitment, the honesty, the sacrifice, and the strong desire which compels a person to express and offer their best to another voluntarily to satisfy a need or a requirement. True love, as referenced above however, operates in three different dimensions in various forms of relationships which requires correspondent responses as follows:

1. The General Expectational Love (GEL).
2. Multifunctional Applied Love (MAL).
3. Exclusive Reciprocal Obligatory Love (EROL).

So far, the General Expectational Love (GEL), the Multifunctional Applied Love (MAL) and the Exclusive Reciprocal Obligatory Love (EROL) are expatiated upon in part three of this book. However, in this chapter, I will treat the Multifunctional Applied Love in more detail and apply its principles to practical and successful marriage. The Multifunctional Applied Love (MAL) is the kind of love which functions in diverse ways and can be applied to various forms of relationships. The MAL dimension is derived from the seven Greek types of love which can be applied to various forms of relationships.

In this context however, I will tailor and apply all the seven Greek types of love to practical marriage love expressions, which are sure to ensure success and happiness in marriage. Spouses by the motivation of their love-need vows are required to express the MAL from the heart in of the intellect, emotions, and volition in three ways:

1. **Expressing Love from the Heart of Intellect** - The MAL dimension of love should be expressed from the heart of the intellect. The heart of the intellect deals with the mind of understanding of the love virtue with its required understanding of its love sacrifices. Spouses must expresses love of virtue to each other by showing forth good and high morals to each other with understanding of its sacrifices and benefits.

2. **Expressing Love from the Heart of Emotions** - The MAL dimension of love should be expressed from the heart of emotions. Spouses must therefore, express love from their emotions or feelings of strong desire, passion, and admiration for each other. The love which is expressed from emotions also protect emotions from negative feeling effects in each other as spouses. In other words, loving with the emotions require spouses to protect each other from negative emotions. The do that by committing not to arouse negative feelings in each other inconsiderately, and intentionally or irresponsibly.

3. **Expressing Love from the Heart of Volition** - The MAL dimension of love should be expressed from

the heart of volition or the will power of decision and commitments. Love must be expressed from the heart of volition or the will to firmly decide and commit to love each other always in both convenient and inconvenient circumstances for lifetime.

Although, expressing love from the emotions is very important in marriage, but for the MAL dimension of love to have its full effects, the spouses must commit to express it from the three dimensions of the heart of the intellect, emotions, and volitions. Hence, the MAL dimension of love must be influenced by the mind of understanding, emotions of strong desire and the volition of decision and commitment.

True love wields a very powerful force and by applying its principles of virtue, spouses shall be empowered to treat each other special to secure each other's happiness. Again, in marriage, love is like the fuel which runs the vehicle of the marriage. Hence, spouses should do well to refuel themselves with all the three dimensions of love so far treated earlier.

If spouses would commit to express love actions toward each other, happiness and success shall not be limited to hopes but an enjoyable reality. The words of the seven Greek types of love in this section are a transliteration from the Greek to English. Spouses are therefore, obliged by their own love-need vows to express the following seven multifunctional applied Greek types of love among the other forms of love treated earlier to each other for lifetime as follows:

(1) Spouses Must Express the Love of Agape to Each Other for Lifetime

Spouses by their own love-need vows are required to express to each other the love of agape The agape expresses unconditional, altruistic, sacrificial, and giving love. It is God's kind of love which does not wait for humanity to show him love or any form of rightness before He shows His love of benevolence and redemption. God is the one who first loved and have been loving all humanity in various ways and forms **(1 John 4:19).**

God by His expression of agape…. *makes His sun rise on the evil and on the good and sends rain on the just and on the unjust* **(Matthew 5:45).** Again, God through Christ Jesus sacrificed Himself to provide salvation for all humanity, especially those who are willing to embrace Jesus as their God and Savior as also affirmed: *For scarcely for a righteous man will one die; yet perhaps for a good man someone would even dare to die. 8 But God demonstrates His own love toward us, in that while* **we were still sinners, Christ died for us** **(Romans 5:7-8).**

Upon the foundation of God's agape, spouses by their love-need vows are also required to express agape to each other for their lifetime. The spouses' expression of agape should include but not limited to the unconditional, altruistic, sacrificial, and giving love of agape to each other as further explained below:

The Unconditional Love of Agape - Spouses should be motivated by their love-need vows to express their unconditional love of agape to each other. By their unconditional love of agape, the spouses are supposed to desire and commit to first offer their best to each other without waiting for the love of the other to be expressed. If the husband and the wife choose to be unconditional in their expression of love to each other, their love needs would be met without any struggle. Again, there should not be the question of who should love first? This is because both the husband and the wife are required by their own love-need vows to love each other first.

1. **The Altruistic Love of Agape** - The love-need vow commitments of the spouses should motivate them to express the altruistic love of agape. The altruistic love of agape of the spouses should motivate them to place each other's interests and needs above their own. Furthermore, spouses should be motivated by their love-need vows to express the altruistic love of agape by showing selfless concern for the wellbeing and happiness of each other as recommended: *Let each of you look out not only for his own interests, but also for the interests of others* **(Philippians 2:4)**.

2. **The Sacrificial Love of Agape** - Again, spouses should be motivated by their love-need vows to express the sacrificial love of agape to each other. Each spouse should be willing to forgo their own

self-interests in order to meet each other's love-needs. The spouses' willingness to sacrifice their own comfort and convenience in order to make each other comfortable as possible, ensures each other's happiness and success of the marriage. Agape love of sacrifice serves as the antidote for the negative ego of selfishness, self-centered, pride, greed, and superiority which hold others in contempt.

3. The Giving Love of Agape - Furthermore, the spouses should be motivated by their own love-need vows to express the giving love of agape. By the giving love of agape, the spouses must be motivated to freely give to each other of whatever is givable, such as their time of attention, care, services, supports, gifts, trust, and protection.

(2) Spouses' Must Express the Love of Philautia to Each Other for Lifetime

Spouse must be motivated by their own love-need vows to express the love of philautia to each other. Philautia is the love of self. Ironically, it is natural to love one's own self ...*For no one ever hates his own flesh, but nourishes and cherishes it, just as the Lord does the church* **(Ephesians 5:29).** Interestingly enough, philautia has two love facets: The unhealthy and healthy love of self. First, the unhealthy love of self is usually expressed in selfishness, self-centeredness, self-indulgence, self-glory, superiority, greed, and arrogance. The chapter one of part six explains in detail the unhealthy love of self under subtopic, "Vow to Leave behind the Intrusions of Ego for Lifetime.

Second, the healthy love of self always desires and seeks to accord to one's own significant spouse the same or more kind of self-nourishment, endearment, respect, and happiness nurtured and applied to self. In marriage, the spouses' love-need vow to love each other for lifetime includes the expression of the healthy self-love of philautia. In expressing philautia, spouses must always remember their love-need vow responsibility to apply the royal law in their marriage as indicated: *If you really fulfill the* **royal law** *according to the Scripture, "You shall* **love your neighbor as yourself***," you do well* (**James 2:8**); And *"Therefore, whatever you want men to* **do to you**, **do also to them**, *for this is the Law and the Prophets* (**Matthew 7:12**).

The willingness and the commitment to apply the royal law is the motivation for spouses to express the healthy and genuine love of philautia to each other. The philautia kind of love is expressed through the placing of high and first premium over the care, nourishment, endearment, protection, and the happiness of each other as spouses as again emphasized in Scripture: *Let nothing be done through* **selfish ambition or conceit**, *but in* **lowliness of mind** *let each* **esteem others better than himself** (Philippians 2:3).

(3) Spouses Must Express Love of Philia to Each Other for Lifetime

Spouse must be motivated by their own love-need vows to express the love of philia to each other. Philia is the love expressed either between brothers or friends. The vow to love each other in marriage requires the genuine expression of philia kind of love to each other as spouses. Marriage love-need vows require the spouses to develop the philia love of close friendship. The philia love expression in marriage should motivate the spouses to become intimate and confidant friends of trust. Developing the confidant friendship of trust motivates the spouses to be transparent, vulnerable, dependable, and a protector of each other's lives for lifetime.

The philia of confidant friendship removes barriers of shame, shyness and fear from marriage which motivates the spouses to trust each other completely. The philia love of confidant friendship in marriage supposed to motivate the spouses to care, share, confide, trust, sacrifice, and become honest partners for mutual life's success enjoyment. Marital philia of confidant friendship also requires spouses to exercise patience toward each other's weaknesses to help each other overcome their own weaknesses. The virtue of patience exhibits tolerance, forgiveness, respect and teachableness of submission to teach and learn from each other.

In philia love of confidant friendship, each spouse is required to make available all their resources of time, strength, knowledge, ideas, wisdom, capabilities, expertise, and finances to ensure the success, and prosperity of the marriage. Genuine expression of philia love of confidant friendship among spouses must lead to the mutual development of closeness, and partnership reliability of trust.

Spouses must commit to solidify their confidant friendship of trust by removing the limits to the free sharing of everything in each other's lives in the marriage without fear, shame or shy. Sharing each other's past must be focused on what can empower the present and future, and where help shall be needed from each other. The things which have the tendency to affect trust and impede the success of marriage should be shared before the marriage. Couples should not hide anything which when discovered in the future can jeopardize the relationship. Couples must give each other the chance to decide on what to expect before the marriage. Sharing of information must be focused on mutual present and future. By the expression of philia, Jesus acknowledged his disciples as friends in these words: *"No longer do I call you servants, for a servant does not know what his master is doing; but I have **called you friends**, for **all things that I heard from My Father I have made known to you** (John 15:15).*

Furthermore, the philia also emphasizes brotherly love. The Scripture recommends the brotherly love to be expressed among all to *…keep on loving one another as brothers and sisters* (**Hebrews13:1**). The spouses are required to motivate themselves by their own love-need vows to express the brotherly love of philia to each other. The expression of brotherly love in marriage requires the spouses to first, share the same values of life. Second, the spouses must mutually own and have all things in common in the marriage. The principle of brotherly love was expressed among the early believers in these words: *Now the multitude of those who believed were of **one heart** and **one soul**; neither did anyone say that any of the things he possessed was his own, but* *they* **had all things in common** **(Acts 4:32)**. The principle of brotherly love which was expressed among the early believers outlines four important qualities:

1. **The Believers were of One Heart** – First, it infers that the first believers united their hearts of conscience with regards to right and wrongs with its cautiousness against hurting each other intentionally. The spouses in expressing their philia love to each other must be cautious against hurting each other intentionally or irresponsibly.

   Second, the believers united their hearts of intuition of sharing ideas and the graces God endowed on them their wellbeing. In brotherly love of philia, the spouses must always commit to share to empower themselves and enhance each other's wellbeing. Third, the believers united their hearts of communion of love and faith toward God the Father, God the Son and God the Holy. It is indeed expedient on spouses to share common faith. Difference in faith can easily develop the potential of distraction to cause divisions in the minds of the spouses.

2. **The Believers were of One Soul** - In other words, their expression of brotherly love, motivated them to unite their soul of intellect, emotions, and volitions in their decisions. First, in expressing brotherly love, the spouses must be motivated to integrate their

mental energies of knowledge, insights, expertise, and wisdom for mutual progress and success in their marriage.

Second, the spouses must be motivated by their brotherly love to integrate their emotional energies. The spouses can integrate their emotional energies by safeguarding their feelings from negative ones in order to desire and admire each intensely. By combining their positive emotions, they can mutually build each other's confidence of beauty, honor, and smartness.

Third, the spouses must be motivated by their brotherly love to integrate their volitional energy of mutual decisions. In mutual principle of decision, the spouses are required to mutually accord each other the courtesy of sharing ideas, agreeing, and deciding on them before execution.

3. The Believers Mutually Owned their Possessions - The believers did not do any self-claim of possessions rather they owned them mutually. Spouses must be motivated by their own love-need vows to desist from claiming things in the marriage for self. When spouses begin to claim things for themselves for whatever reason, they have initiated an unrealized separation in the heart which will hurt their marital relationship in the course of time.

4. The Believers had all Things in Common. Spouses by the motivation of their own love-need vows are required to have all things in common in the marriage. In other words, spouses should be motivated by their love to pull all their resources together in order to achieve greater things in their lives and marriage to be mutually enjoyed.

(4) Spouses Must Express Love of Pragma to Each Other for Lifetime

Spouses must be motivated by their own love-need vows to express the love of pragma to each other sincerely and cheerfully. Pragma is the love of endurance, long-suffering, and long-lasting. It is the practical, and realistic love based on responsibility and commitment. Genuine love of pragma should motivate loving spouses to cheerfully stand the life's test of time of convenience and inconvenience in the journey of the marriage. The spouses' vow to love each other for lifetime includes the expression of pragma of endurance, long-suffering and long-lasting. Pragma in marriage is developed out of the process of maturing in love through patience, commitment, knowledge, understanding and experience. The love of pragma in marriage can be expressed in three major ways as stated above:

Firstly, the spouses must be motivated by their own love-need vows to express the pragma love of endurance to each other. They must be willing to commit to growing together in the pragma love of endurance in three ways:

1. **Endurance Love of Tolerance** - The love-need vows of the spouses should motivate them to commit to grow together in the endurance love of tolerance. It is extremely important for the spouses to develop their love of endurance of tolerance because they are not perfect. The spouses' human imperfections may at times surface to cause them to fall short of pleasing each other as expected. As a result, the spouses must be ready to tolerate and help each other grow out of their weaknesses. Failure to make the necessary efforts to grow out of weaknesses in order to please each other in the marriage is bound to cause a lot of hurts to each other.

2. **Endurance Love of Patience** - Since marriage is a lifetime journey, it will require patience to ensure success and happiness. Patience can be defined comprehensively from biblical perspective as the willingness and the commitment to tolerate the slow and long process of life, bearing with weaknesses of others, criticisms, delays, irritating situations, troubling circumstances, and suffering calmly, without feeling hostile and compromising virtue or high good morals.

   Endurance of patience in marriage is cardinal to marital success because it takes patience to develop the bond of cleaving in marriage. First, marital cleaving requires the spouses to commit to stick together their intellect which is their minds of perceptions and opinions. Second, they must commit to stick together and responsibly manage their emotions by safeguarding against the arousal of negative feelings in each other. Third, the spouse must be ready to join their volitions of deciding powers and preferences. Fourth, the spouses must commit to stick together their conscience by understanding the effects of right and wrong actions and attitudes in marriage. Again, the spouses should commit to cleave their intuitions by sharing, owning, and utilizing each other's visionary, creative and innovative, ideas for mutual progress and benefits.

3. **Endurance Love of Perseverance** - The love-need vows of the spouses again, should motivate them to commit to grow together in the pragma love of endurance which nurtures perseverance in the spouses. The virtue of perseverance is what helps the spouses to nurture each other into the desired and attractive spouse they both expect.

Secondly, the spouses must motivate themselves by their own love-need vows to express to each other the pragma love of long-suffering. The spouses must commit to grow together in their pragma love of long-suffering. Long-suffering requires the spouses to express the virtues of forbearance, forgiveness, and empathy as follows:

1. **Long-Suffering Love of Forbearance** - Spouse by their own motivation of love-need vows should commit to express to each other the long-suffering love of forbearance. The motivation of forbearance causes the spouses to exercise self-control against reactive behaviors and utterance which results in greater hurts and irreparable regrets. The motivation of the love of forbearance requires spouses to exercise self-control over their mind, emotions and will in order not to give in to their own weaknesses to hurt each other. The expression of the love of forbearance also requires the spouses to develop courage in adversities which may come in the course of the marriage.

2. **Long-Suffering Love of Forgiveness** - The spouses should be motivated by their own love-need vows to express the long-suffering love of forgiveness. Forbearing each other and developing a daily sharing of concerns, displeasures, offences, hurts, and general experiences are very vital to the health of the marriage. It is highly commendable for spouses to address all concerns and experiences in each day and see to forgive where necessary and unite their spirits by praying together before retiring to bed. Developing the habit to resolve all misunderstanding, displeasures, and grudges daily require mutual submission from each as the Scripture affirms: ... *submitting to one another in the fear of God* (**Ephesians 5:21**).

3. **Long-Suffering Love of Empathy** - Moreover, the spouses love-need vows should motivate them to express the long-suffering love of empathy to each other. By the long-suffering love of empathy, the spouses are required to express their deep concern, understanding and a relieving care to each other. The spouses must always be ready to express understanding, show concern, care and provide comforting supports in all stressful moments in each other's life.

Thirdly, the spouses should motivate themselves by their own love-need vows to express to each other the pragma of long-lasting love. Long-lasting love requires the spouses to commit to always give, sacrifice, admire, nourish, cherish, and protect each other for lifetime. In long-lasting love of pragma, spouses' love actions must not be a nine-day wonder; rather, their long-lasting love should last for their lifetime.

By long-lasting love of pragma, the spouses are required to make all the necessary efforts to adjust to each other and the new life of the marriage. In doing so, the spouses shall be assured of their own happiness in the new life of marriage. In fact, the quicker the spouses are able to adjust from their ego of selfishness, selfishness, pride, and greed to the new life of the marriage, the better the enjoyment of their marriage. The commitment to express the long-lasting love of pragma in marriage, enforces and ensures the compatibility of agreement among the spouses as asked in Scripture: *Can two people walk together without agreeing on the direction* **(Amos 3:3 NLT)**?

(5) Spouses Must Express Love of Ludus to Each Other for Lifetime

The spouses' vow to love each other for a lifetime include ludus. Ludus is the playful, child-like, and fun kind of loving each other. Spouses are required to motivate themselves by their love-need vows to express to each other the love of ludus. In expressing the love of ludus, the spouses must commit to remain vulnerable, humble, flexible, playful, jovial, and easygoing in order for ludus to be enjoyed. Again, the love-need vows of the spouses should motivate them to enjoy the child-like, playfulness and fun in their marriage. The spouses can freely express and enjoy the marital ludus by creating the atmosphere of casualness, carefreeness, shamelessness, and shylessness.

In fact, creating the conducive atmosphere of casualness in marriage is perfect way for the spouses to expression their love of ludus. The intentional creation of casualness in marital relationship helps to remove the fear of condemnation, condescension, disrespect, and shyness. In fact, Adam and his wife were naked without shame or shy **(Genesis 2:25);** and nothing should create shame or shyness among spouses if they really desire to enjoy the ludus fun love in marriage. Spouses must do well not to grow above their childish nostalgias. Loving spouses should do well not to let go of their childish nostalgia of fun and playfulness.

Furthermore, the love of ludus should motivate spouses to engage in intentional flirting, and sexual teasing to spice up their love of romance and intimacy. Again, the love of ludus should motivate the spouses to create the atmosphere of complete freedom to talk and discuss sex with fun and excitement. Spouse can only enjoy the love of ludus if they will be ready to express their love of ludus freely without fear, shame, and shyness. If the spouses show any demeaning sign for each other to feel being perceived as evil, spoiled or a profaner, the fire of ludus will be quenched completely.

When the spouses remove the love of ludus from their marriage, everything shall become very formal and rigid, and such atmosphere shall not augur well for the happiness of the spouses. In marriage, there should be no conversation or portrayals among the spouses which should be considered as profane or unholy. Spouses should never forget that the very essence of ludus is all about removing love barriers from their marriage in order to give way for love freedom of expression without restrictions. The giving of chance to each other to freely express the fun and playful love of ludus, removes fear, shame, and shyness from marriage. The free expression of the love of ludus empowers the spouses to enjoy love in its informalities of playfulness and fun manner like children.

(6) Spouses Must Express Love of Storge to Each Other for Lifetime

The love-need vows of spouses supposed to motivate them to express to each other the love of storge for their lifetime. Storge is the love expressed among family; thus, between parents and their children, and between siblings and siblings. First, the love of storge is what motivates parents to express their love of care, endearment, nourishment, provision, protection, coaching, and planning for a better future for their children.

In the same manner, spouses as a family for lifetime, should be motivated by their love-need vows to express the love of storge to each other. The storge love should compel the spouses to express the mutual love of care, endearment, nourishment, provision, protection, coaching, and planning together for a better future that can be mutually enjoyed. The caution however is that the spouses should be careful not to parade themselves as each other's parents to treat each other as children. The treatment of each other in the relationship manner of parent and child depicts an attitude of disrespect.

By divine order of marriage, spouses are equal partners. However, the husband is required to be a servant, responsible and accountable leader for his marital home. Interestingly enough, it was Eve, the wife of Adam who first ate from the forbidden tree and even influenced her husband to also eat, but Adam was held responsible because he was the leader. In fact, in marriage, the husband is required of God to assume responsibilities for his family. This is because as the responsible servant leader, he shall give account of his marriage and children before God; and then followed by his wife.

Second, siblings are required by blood to love each other by caring, protecting, sharing, helping, and holding each other accountable. By the same token, spouses are required by their own love-need vows to express their storge love of caring, sharing, protecting, helping, and holding each other accountable. Spouses should not be motivated by their ego of selfishness, self-centeredness, jealousy, greed, and arrogance to neglect their responsibility toward each other. Cain however, replaced his love of storge toward his brother Abel with hate in these words: *Then the LORD said to Cain,* **"where is Abel your brother?"** *He said,* **"I do not know. Am I my brother's keeper?"** *10 And He said, "What have you done? The voice of your brother's blood cries out to Me from the ground* (**Genesis 4:9,10**).

Third, children are also required to return the love of storge toward their parents. Although, there are many out there who are from dysfunctional families who do not operate in responsible love for each other. However, loving each other as family by caring, providing, helping, and protecting each other is God's ideal plan for families as stated: *Children with good sense make their parents happy, but foolish children despise them.* (**Proverbs 15:20, CEV**).

In the same manner, spouses by their love-need vows are required to express the storge love of care, endearment, nourishment, protection, helping, coaching, providing, and planning with each other to secure a better future for mutual enjoyment. However, the expression of storge must be reciprocal and mutual because it cannot be fulfilled and enjoyed one-sidedly in marriage. If either the husband or the wife fails to fulfill their love responsibility of storge to the other, it shall tilt the love scale out of balance to cause hurts and heartbreaks among spouses.

(7) Spouses Must Express Love of Eros to Each Other for Lifetime

Marriage by its love-need vows obligates the spouses to express the love of eros to each other for their lifetime. The eros in marriage is simply about the erotic or sexual love which must be expressed among the spouses. The spouses by the motivation of their love-need vows are required to commit to fulfill each other's sexual needs without to beg for it. Spouses must realize that their sexual desires are emotional delicate needs which must be fulfilled for each other mutually. Scripture affirms that sexual needs are real needs, and it is metaphorically described as a burning fire which requires the spouses to quench it for each other when needed as affirmed: … but if they cannot exercise self-control, let them marry. *For it is better to marry than to burn with passion* (**1 Corinthians 7:9**).

Marriage enrolls the spouses in the erotic love, and it empower them to serve each other cheerfully as intimate or sexual-need desire-fire extinguishing spouses. The spouses are obligated by their own love-need vows to quench each other's erotic thirst. The enjoyment of eros in marriage in its emotional, and bodily euphoric is the pathway to bonding in body, mind, and emotions. Surprisingly, sex is the only ecstatic activity which bonds the two bodies into one flesh as affirmed in the caution against sexual sins: *Or do you not know that he who is **joined*** (in sex) **to a harlot is one body with her? For *"the two,"* He says, *"shall become one flesh* (1 Corinthians 6:16; Genesis 2:24).**

One of God's design purposes of sex is to bond the two engaging spouses into oneness of flesh and spirit. The sexual oneness bonding is activated through the euphoric brain release of its bonding love hormone of oxytocin. The bonding oneness of the spouses partly results from the release of the oxytocin love hormone from the brain into the body. The oxytocin bonding love hormone gets released into the body of the spouses through their romantic cuddling and orgasmic sexual intercourse. The oxytocin love hormone helps to deepen the unexplainable feeling of closeness and attachment of the spouses.

Sex outside marriage is biblically considered a sin for several reasons. First, it is sacred in the sense that God has set it apart to be fully enjoyed in the confines and safety of marriage. Consequently, one can attest to fact that a break in sexual relationship outside marriage still causes great hurt and bitterness among the partners. The reason is that sex enjoins the two-engaging couple with the oxytocin and other emotional, mental, and spiritual mechanisms. In fact, sex does not only bond the body, but it also bonds what is inside the body. In other words, sex bonds the two engaging minds, emotions and influences the volitions with its decision powers of the spouses.

Sexual love expressed in marriage should motivate genuine love of selflessness, admiration, and strong attraction for each other. The spouses must always remember that their eros or erotic love should be freely given and enjoyed by each other mutually. The lifetime love-need vows should motivate the spouses to make the expression of their erotic sexual love unrestricted and unscheduled. But rather, the spouses should be creative by being intentional to plan, seduce, satisfy, and be spontaneous in their sexual love expressions as proof of each other's strong desire and attraction toward each other.

Genuine erotic love should generate in each spouse a sense of oneness and belonging as affirmed in Scripture by the Shulamite, king Solomon's wife in these words: *I am my beloved's, and his desire is toward me* (**Song 7:10**). Interestingly enough, the two names: Solomon and Shulamite share the same meaning as peaceful or peaceable. As a result, both can be addressed as Mr. & Mrs. Peaceful. In fact, Song of Songs portray a lot of their romantic and intimate love expressions in a beautiful poetic and euphemistic style of which some requires decoding in order to understand. As already emphasized, eros love of sex is the main engagement which makes two bodies into one flesh according to Scripture (**Genesis 2:24**).

The One-Flesh Principle of Marriage

The one-fleshness in marriage is the consummation level of the marriage by which the one-flesh covenant reaches its apex as stated: *Therefore, a man shall leave his father and mother and be joined to his wife, and they shall become* ***one flesh*** (Genesis 2:24). Marriage without sex, renders it incomplete and unfulfilled because the two bodies shall never reach its state of one-fleshness. There cannot be a celibate marriage and if there should be, it shall be reduced to only a caring relationship as realized between the old king David and his beautiful young virgin wife Abishag as declared in the following statement: *The young woman was very lovely; and **she cared for the king and served him**; but the king **did not know her*** (**1Kings 1:4**).

The word "know" is used several times in the Bible to describe sexual engagement among spouses as follows: *Now Adam **knew** Eve his wife, and **she conceived** and bore Cain, and said, "I have acquired a man from the LORD* (**Genesis 4:1**);"... *And Elkanah **knew** Hannah his wife, and the **LORD remembered her*** (**1Samuel 1:19**). The Hebrew word "know" in certain context is used euphemistically to reference sexual relations. King David as referenced earlier, married the young virgin Abishag, lived together as spouses in his old age, but he could not know her intimately or sexually. As a result, their marital relationship could not reach its apex of one-fleshness through sexual intercourse.

Sex, therefore, must be freely given and willingly received or enjoyed, to establish the eros love commitment as a proof of bonding, strong attraction, and strong desire for each other as spouses. Sex must be fun and free flowing among spouses. The reason is that first, it establishes the marriage by its bonding power. Second, it brings physical health to the bodies of the spouses. Third, it brings health to the spirits of the spouses' minds, and emotions which brings about clarity of focus to ensure their right and viable decisions in the marriage.

In fact, one of the signs of a dying attraction and passion in marriage is the dwindling of sexual love expressions in marriage for whatever reasons they may be. Consequently, when the spouses' ego of selfishness, self-centeredness, extreme jealousy, pride, and greed intrude the marriage, it will begin to affect the spouses' sexual love expressions. The intrusion of ego usually overthrows the spouses' love of care, endearment, nourishment, attention, giving, sacrifice, and protection to begin the marital decline.

Hence, the spouses' love-need vows, should motivate them to safeguard their marriage against their ego's intrusion; or else, their sexual love shall dwindle to begin a spiral decline of their marital relationship. Furthermore, the spouses' love-need vow commitment to fulfill each other's sexual needs demands a forfeiture of authority over each other's bodies as affirmed: *The wife does not have authority over her own body, but the husband does. And likewise, the husband does not have authority over his own body, but the wife does* (**1Corintians 7:4**).

Understanding and embracing the mutual sex enjoyment and bonding principle in marriage should be the way for the spouses to intentionally attract, admire, desire, and engage each other sexually as confirmed in Scripture: *My people are destroyed for lack of knowledge…* (**Hosea 4:6**). The importance of sex in marriage should never be downplayed and the spouses should be intentional in safeguarding their sexual love against any intrusions of ego. A caution though, is that the spouses should be careful not to use sex as bargaining chip or punishing blow against each other; for such habit will not augur well for the flourishing of the marital relationship. Instead, the spouses must see to resolve conflicts and settle their misunderstanding than to use them to deny each other of sex as a form of punishment.

Denying each other of sex in marriage is a violation of the sexual love-need vow which requires sexual authority exchange among the spouses after marriage. The spouses in effect, are required to commit to express the love of eros to each other intentionally for their mutual satisfaction and bonding. Spouses must, therefore, do well to avoid depriving each other of sex, because it does not solve a marital conflict. It rather escalates the conflict and causes emotional separation which when not intervene may gradually lead to physical separation.

Consequently, if the spouses refuse to fix the causes of their conflicts, it will gradually lead to physical separation and subsequent decline of the marriage. It must, however, be noted that denying each other of sex alone is not the only act which causes emotional separation in marriage. But rather, the motivations of ego which refuses to fulfill each other's love-need required vows to each other. The selfish refusal to meet each other's general, emotional, and physical love-needs to each other is the core contributing factor of decline of marriage.

CHAPTER THREE

VOW TO FULFILL THE FIVE NEEDS OF COMPANIONSHIP FOR LIFETIME

*Yet you say, "For what reason?" Because the LORD has been witness between you and the wife of your youth, with whom you have **dealt treacherously**; Yet she is your **companion** and **your wife by covenant** (Malachi 2:14).*

The marriage love-need vows require the spouses to fulfill to each other five needs of companionship to enhance their marital relationship. The marriage love-need vows should always remind all spouses of their companionship responsibilities toward each other. Marital companionship requires the spouses to commit to fulfill five major needs in the marriage to ensure success and happiness in the marriage.

The five major needs of marital companionship include but not limited to partnership, confidant-friendship, attention, complementarity, and togetherness:

(1) Spouses Must Commit to The Companionship of Partnership

In marital companionship of partnership, each spouse is required to commit to the marriage the hundred percent of their lives and love; but not fifty percent. There are many who agree to marry but, in their heart, they are only willing to bring fifty percent of their lives and love commitment to test the waters of the marital relationship. To only offer fifty percent of one's life and love to marriage means, the person has only one foot in the marriage and the other is outside the marriage.

Partial commitment to the love-need vows of marriage, shall neither produce success nor happiness in marriage. Genuine and sincere candidates of marriage should be willing to give themselves completely to their marriage and commit to fulfill their love-need vows of marriage to ensure success and happiness.

When God brought the first woman into marriage, He required her to give hundred percent of her cable help to Adam, her husband in order for him to be fulfilled **(Genesis 2:18).** In general, the capable love-help responsibilities of wives are the things which make their husbands absolutely fulfilled in their marital life. The wife's indispensable love-help in marriage includes but not limited to providing the absolute necessary support, care, respect, nourishment, endearment, attention, services, comfort, guidance, and solutions to her husband.

Adam on the other hand, received Eve, his wife with the commitment to give his hundred percent of acceptance, admiration, care, honor, nourishment, endearment, attention, services, comfort, guidance, and solutions to her. Adam expressed his love-need vow commitment to treat his wife as his very bone of bones and flesh of his own flesh **(Genesis 2:23).** In other words, every good thing a husband may desire for himself, the same and better must first be given to his wife out of the motivation of love and vice versa.

Spouses must, therefore, by their love-need vows should be motivated to fulfill their companionship of partnership needs to ensure their own the success and prosperity. Again, by the motivation of their love-need vows, the spouses must commit to their marriage, the hundred percent of their lives and love in order to bring about great results and success in the marriage.

Furthermore, spouses must realize that the withholding of any part of their love and life's resources from the marriage, shall inadvertently, impede their marital success and stifle their own happiness. Partial commitment of life and love investment in marriage, signifies that the spouses are not in the marriage to combine resources in partnership for mutual prosperity. But rather, they are in the marriage to utilize their spouses' resources to build their own future prosperity. The fifty percent attitude is an intrusion of ego to destroy the marital relationship.

Marital hundred percent commitment to the companionship of partnership, multiplies the resources of the spouses to achieve greater successes for mutual enjoyment. When spouses commit to their own love-need vows to fulfill each other in partnership, and combine resources to secure their future success, happiness shall be a reality and not a dream. In true marital partnership, where each spouse offers up hundred percent of their life and love's commitment, their efforts shall make the unachievable achievable in the marriage. Marital companionship does not only require partnership, but it also requires confidant-friendship.

(2) Spouse Must Commit to Companionship of Confidant-Friendship

Spouses by their love-need vows, should be motivated to nurture their companionship of confidant-friendship in their marriage. Companionship of confidant-friendship in marriage can be described as the close relationship and mutual admiration between the husband and the wife, which is characterized by commitment to complete transparency, admiration, trust, vulnerability, reliability, support, and protection. Companionship of confidant-friendship, should motivate the spouses to exhibit the following qualities toward each other:

1. **Confidant-Friendship is Characterized by Complete Transparency** - The marital love-need vows should motivate the spouses toward

complete transparency in their companionship of confidant-friendship. The unique confidant-friendship in marital relationship supposed to empower the spouses to nurture closeness, intimacy, and nakedness among each other. The complete transparency in confidant-friendship, requires the spouses to commit to be mentally, emotionally, and physically naked in every way possible in order to avoid surprises, disappointments, and hurts. If spouses commit to develop their relationship into confidant-friendship, it will help the spouses to be comfortable and vulnerable without fear, shame and shy.

2. **Confidant-Friendship is Characterized by Admiration** – The love-need vows should motivate the spouses to nurture admiration for each other in order to maintain mutual irresistibility among the spouses. Spousal admiration does not happen automatically; but rather it is an intentional effort to see and appreciate the beauty and virtues in, on and around each other as confidant befriended spouses.

3. **Confidant-Friendship is Characterized by Trust** - Companionship of confidant-friendship in marriage requires the spouses to give each other every reason to trust each other. Marital confidant-friendship should do away with secrets and make each other predictable. Spouses must understand that lies

betray trust, and the Bible cautions against it in this way: *But let your **'yes' be 'yes,' and your 'no,' 'no.'** For whatever is more than these is from the <u>evil one</u>* **(Matthew 5:37).**

Confidant-friendship of trust should alleviate fear of reasonable doubts among spouses as also affirmed: *There is no fear in love; but perfect love casts out fear, because fear involves torment. But he who fears has not been made perfect in love* **(1John 4:18).** Spouses are required by their own love-need vows to express the perfect love of complete honesty to each other in order to make the marital relationship fear-free. Spousal dishonesty creates fear among themselves to destroy their marital love. If spouses give reasons for distrust, they have in actuality rendered their love imperfect to cause marital tensions. The imperfecting of marital love with distrust and dishonesty cause fear of both mental and emotional torment in each other.

4. **Confidant-Friendship is Characterized by Vulnerability** - The love-need vows of marriage require the spouses to encourage confidant-friendship of vulnerability which transitions the spouses from self-protection to mutual protection. The spousal development of complete confidant-friendship of vulnerability, removes the fear of attack or harm from each other. Marital confidant-friendship of vulnerability should give each other the reason for safety

and future security. There should be no circumstance by which the spouses should react in anger, hostility and to abuse each other verbally or physically. Inconsiderate behaviors like this shall cause the weaker one to transition to self-protective mode to close up all doors into his or her heart. The Scripture cautions against threatful behaviors with these words: *The Lord's bond-servant must not be* **quarrelsome**, *but be* **kind to all**, *skillful in teaching,* **patient when wronged**… **(2 Timothy .2:24, NASB)**

5. **Confidant-Friendship is Characterized by Reliability** - The marital love-need vow of confidant-friendship should always motivate reliability among the spouses. The confidant-friendship of reliability in marriage emphasizes authentic and consistent life qualities which challenge the spouses not to disappoint each in character. In other words, the spouses by their love motivations should give each other all the reasons to rely on and to depend on each other's good and promising character and behavior.

6. **Confidant-Friendship is Characterized by Support** - In marital confidant-friendship, the spouses are required by the reason of their own love-need vows to give every support each one may need from each other always. The spouses must commit to give every needed emotional, mental, physical, and gen-

eral life support to each other in both convenient and inconvenient circumstances.

7. **Confidant-Friendship is Characterized by Protection** - Furthermore, companionship of confidant-friendship actually demands of the spouses to commit to each other's mental, emotional, and physical protection. Marital confidant-friendship, should therefore, safeguard each other from attitudinal, verbal, and physical abuses. The reason being that attitudinal, verbal, and physical abuses, adversely affect the health of the mind, emotions, and the physical wellbeing of each spouse. Spouses must also see to protect each other from inside and outside forces of danger as a proof of confidant-friendship commitment to each other.

Consequently, developing commitment for marital companionship of confidant-friendship shall move the marriage to a great level of closeness, happiness, trust, fondness, and complete dependability. Just as *a friend loves at all times…* **(Proverbs 17:17),** confidant friends in marriage are required to express their love of friendship at all convenient and inconvenient times. At this level of confidant-friendship, the marriage becomes free from secrets and privacies.

Again, becoming confidant friends in marriage, require the spouses to trust each other with their lives, love, and confidentialities, being motivated by trust, and reliance.

There should be no circumstance by which marital trust should be betrayed either in secret or in public to others because of the spouses' own vows to remain as confidant friends for lifetime. The spouses should motivate themselves by their own love-need vows to not betray each other's trust with infidelities.

Finally, one may ask, when should marital relationship reach this level of confidant-friendship? In fact, before, a couple ties the knot of marriage, they should have developed a remarkable close, honest, reliable, and true friendship of trust to set the pace for continuous confidant-friendship in their marriage. Before, a couple decides to marry, they should have to screen their relationship of all signs of habitual marital success and happiness impediments of dishonesty, distrust, disrespect, intransparence, selfishness, self-centeredness, pride, and stinginess.

The marital success and happiness impediments should cause a person to think twice before deciding to marry such a person. Many a times, people allow themselves to go blind as a bat with the motivation of so-called blind love. To some, it is expedient to give love benefit of doubts to the doubted. However, the so-called love benefit of doubt has always ended up in disappointment, hurts and heartbreaks.

(3) Spouses Must Commit to Companionship of Attention

The marital love-need vows of marriage, require spousal commitment to the companionship of attention.

The companionship of attention in marriage requires the spouses to notice, regard, care, listen, and heed to each other as follows:

1. **Companionship Attention of Noticing** - The love-need vows of marriage require the spouses to commit to the companionship attention of noticing each other in order to appreciate what each other portrays and do around each other. Noticing and appreciating each other's efforts, good works and good looks or attractiveness are some of the ways to prove each other's companionship of attention as spouses.

    However, when spouses invest time, money, and efforts to please each other in good works and good looks without being noticed and appreciated, the spouses shall interpret it as meanness or lack of love. In life, everyone loves to have a cheering; and in marriage, the spouses are required by their own love-need vows to serve as each other's cheerleader. Spousal cheerleading is required to empower and encourage each other to do and offer their best to each other in the marriage.

2. **Companionship Attention of Regard** - The Love-need vows of marriage require the spouses to commit to the companionship attention of regard for each other. The expression of gratitude, friendliness, respect and holding each other in high esteem are some of the ways of giving attention of regard to each other in marriage.

3. **Companionship Attention of Care** - The marital companionship of attention requires the spouses to exhibit special care and treatment of each other. The spouses love-need vow commitments should motivate the spouses to search for every opportunity to express their loving care and special treatments of each other in any way possible. If spouses would think and meditate on ways to express their special care and treatment of each other, so many ideas shall begin to flow into each other's mind. Meditating on how to care and treat each other special causes each other's presence to be established in the minds of each other as loving spouses.

4. **Companionship Attention of Listening** - The love-need vows require the spouses to express their marital companionship of attention through attentive listening to each other's important and so-called unimportant concerns, and conversations. When it comes to marital conversation, no topic of discussion should be termed as unimportant. Anything any spouse talks about is important to that spouse, and the other spouse by the motivation of love should show forth attentive listening without criticism and the loss of focus.

    The companionship of attention supposed to encourage attentiveness toward honest, and unrestricted conversations among spouses. When it comes to spousal conversations, there should be nothing called profane among each other in marriage. In fact, spouses must allow themselves to talk about their sexual lives freely and express their desires for each other without the feeling of shame or shyness.

5. **Companionship Attention of Heed** - Again, with regards to the companionship of attention, the spouses are required by their own love-need vows to heed to each other in any way possible. In marriage, the spouses are required to be accountable to each other and keeper of each other. Hence, the spouses have the responsibility to be each other's advisor by way guiding themselves toward the right ways of life. That is why submission to each other in marriage is a requirement for marital success and spousal happiness as affirmed: ... *submitting to one another in the fear of God* (**Ephesians 5:21**).

When spouses refuse to heed to each other's advice, they have set their pace toward regrettable troubles of life. Since marriage makes the husband and his wife one in everything, whatever happens to one shall also affect the other. Hence, for the spouses' own sake, they have to motivate themselves by their love-need vows to heed to each other's laudable advice and cautions.

Now therefore, if spouses would enjoy their marriage, they must commit their hundred percent attention to each other intentionally by noticing each other's needs and concerns and providing the necessary caring and listening attention to each other. If spouses would commit to open their eyes and ears to each other's needs and concerns, they shall be known and fulfilled easily without being told. Spouses must always think about each other's needs and ask themselves, what each can do to care and meet those needs without being asked? Spouses are therefore, required not to underestimate each other's concerns and needs no matter what it is when they are expressed.

During conversation, spouses should be careful not to categorize information to what deserves attention and what does not. The reason is that when it comes to marital companionship of attention, everything is important to the spouse communicating or sharing those concerns. Showing signs of inattentiveness is considered unloving, careless, and insensitive to each other's emotions and needs. In moments of sharing, spouses must prove love and care by focusing on their spouse, looking into the eyes, and showing full attention to their concerns during conversation.

(4) Spouses Must Commit to Companionship of Complementarity

And if they were all one member, where would the body be? 20 But now indeed there are many members, yet one body. 21 And the eye cannot say to the hand, "I have no need of you". nor again the head to the feet,"I have no need of you **(1 Corinthians 12:19-21)."**

The love-need vows of spouses should motivate them to commit to the companionship of complementarity. The word complementarity is from the word complete and by that the spouses are giving the opportunity to complete or bring perfection to each other and the relationship. If spouses commit to marital complementarity, they shall never lack any good thing in all areas of their lives as affirmed: *But let patience have its perfect work, that you may be perfect and* **complete, lacking nothing.** **(James 1:4).**

God from the beginning of life, created the heterosexual couple to make each other complete with their various uniqueness, qualities, and strengths in order not for them to lack any good thing in their marriage as affirmed in these words: *And the LORD God said, "It is not good that man should be alone; I will make him* **a helper comparable to him** *(Genesis 2:18)."* The word comparable or suitable help in marriage, portrays the complementarity principle as stated above.

One of the essences of the heterosexual marriage is derived from the divine principle of completeness. In the principle of complementarity, both the husband and the wife are required to bring all their unique abilities, capabilities, and strengths to the marriage to make life easy for each other and the marriage successful. If the spouses would acknowledge and serve each other with their uniqueness, abilities, capabilities, and strengths, their marriage shall lack no good thing as God intended it.

The Marital companionship of complementarity should remind each spouse of their own incompleteness, imperfections, and lacks. Due to the general human insufficiencies, the spouses must acknowledge that they owe each other what makes each other complete and fulfilled in their marriage as recommended in these words: *Owe no one anything except to love one another, for he who loves another has fulfilled the law* **(Romans 13:8).** The principle here affirms that what each one owes to each other is love.

The application of this principle to marriage, makes the husband and his wife, love indebted to each other. The spouses' self-debt of love requires them by the motivation of their vow to make love payments to each other for their lifetime. Love has the compelling motivation to perfect each other's weaknesses and fulfill each other in every desired good thing of life. Spouses must therefore, come to the realization that they owe each other love of the love which has capacity and propensity to make each other complete, successful, and fulfilled. Hence spouses should always remind themselves not to slack to express love or be late in expressing love to each other for it is their lifetime debt toward each. Commitment to the love of complementarity shall motivate the spouses to commit to pay their love due to supplement each other's lacks to make each other complete and fulfilled as marital companions.

Understanding and committing to apply the principle of complementarity, empowers each spouse to be strong, adequate, and complete in their places of lack and weakness. Our Lord Jesus assured Apostle Paul of His grace and strength in his weakness as stated: *And He said to me, "My grace is sufficient for you, for My strength is made perfect in* weakness." *Therefore, most gladly I will rather boast in my infirmities, that the power of Christ may rest upon me* **(2 Corinthians 12:9).** Finally, spouses must motivate themselves by their own love-need vows to assure and commit to empower themselves with each other's strengths to make each other complete, lacking nothing in the marital companionship.

(5) Spouses Must Commit to Companionship of Togetherness

> ***Two are better than one***, *because they have a **good reward for their labor.**[10] For if they **fall**, **one will lift up his companion***. *But woe to him who is alone when he falls*, *for he has **no one to help him up*** **(Ecclesiastes 4:9,10).**

Furthermore, marital companionship does not only require partnership, confidant-friendship, attention, and complementarity, but it also requires togetherness. The spouses must, therefore, commit to the companionship of togetherness by the motivation of their own love-need vows of marriage. Companionship of togetherness is expedient and required in every marriage because it provides the marriage with diverse and unique resources which reduces the burdens of life to ensure greater success and happiness.

When spouses commit to the companionship of togetherness, they will enjoy their collective personal resources of time, energy, knowledge, skills, finances, and the heterosexual unique strengths and abilities. Interestingly enough, when the husband and his wife commit to their companionship of togetherness, they double all their resources for greater achievements and success because *two are **better than one**, because they have a **good reward for their labor* (Eccleciates 12:9)**. Togetherness in marital companionship has seven benefits:

1. When the spouses commit to combine their resources, their marital achievements and success become very great for mutual benefits and enjoyment.
2. The spouses' togetherness reinforces their physical, mental, and emotional protection against outside marital threats.
3. The spouses' togetherness secures their future against all odds of life because they have each other and God.
4. The togetherness in marriage helps to sharpen the spouses to become the best version of themselves spiritually, mentally, emotionally, volitionally, morally, and potentially because they have become each other's resource for the betterment of their lives.
5. The spouses who commit to the companionship of togethers are able to secure themselves against discouragements because they have become each other's motivation and source of encouragement and courage.
6. Spouses in committed togetherness can be assured of making right decisions in life and marriage because it is said that "two heads are better than one."

7. The companionship of togetherness alleviates aloneness which leads to loneliness. The spouses' togetherness enhances their oneness, intimacy, and beautiful romance in their marriage.

Therefore, the spouses, who are willing to achieve the best of life, and be able to enjoy each other, must commit to the companionship of partnership, confidant-friendship, attention, complementarity, and togetherness.

CHAPTER FOUR

VOW TO KEEP THE MARRIAGE BED PURE FOR LIFETIME

Marriage is honorable among all, and the bed undefiled; but fornicators and adulterers God will judge
(Hebrews 13:4).

Marriage by divine order, requires the spouses to fulfill their love-need vows to keep their marriage bed pure for lifetime. The biblical verse above cautions against the defilement of the marriage bed. The bed emphasized in this verse is not the recliner or the physical bed spouses sleep on. The bed in reference is a Greek euphemistic word which is transliterated as "koite." In this context, the word koite refers to the process by which sperm is deposited into the womb through sex. It could also mean the sexual organs of both the male and the female which ejaculates and receives the semen or the spermatozoa respectively. A similar word from a Latin origin is coitus which means copulation or sexual intercourse. The implication of this verse emphasizes four major principles of conjugal sexual privileges:

First, marriage is universally considered as honorable, thus, worthy of universal respect by everyone. Indeed, marriage is highly regarded in high esteem by all ethnic groups, and all nations of the world. Spouses by their love-need vows are therefore, required to honor each other in the marriage and respect its marital principles and commitments. The spouses' commitment to fulfill their love-need vows to each other is the way to honor the institution of marriage. To fail to fulfill the required love-need vows of marriage is an intentional way of dishonoring the institution of marriage.

Second, the marriage bed is sacred and has been set aside or reserved in marriage to fulfill the sexual needs of the husband and his wife alone. Marital sexual life is a privilege God has given to the spouses to enjoy without reservation and feeling of any form of guilt. Therefore, the expression of sexual intimacy in marriage is indeed very pure and it's endorsed by God.

Third, the Scripture warns against fornication, which is the abuse of the male and the female sexual organs through any form of sexual activities outside the confines of marriage. The implication is that fornication is a perversion and an abuse of God's plan of sexual intercourse. Therefore, God has designated fornication to incur His judgment because it destroys its designated divine purposes.

Fourth, spouses are cautioned by God not to defile their sexual organs in any way or form outside their marriage. In other words, the conjugal or the marital sexual privileges are not supposed to be shared with any other person outside the marriage. The reason is that the marriage bed which euphemistically represents the sexual organs and the sexual communication between the husband, and the wife are exclusive to them alone. The sacredness of sex and its marital exclusivity is beautifully and metaphorically emphasized in Proverbs chapter five and verses fifteen through twenty. However, the entire chapter five warns against the pitfalls of immorality. I shall, however, interpret those referenced verses of Scripture in the light of the spouses' love-need vow to keep their marriage bed pure for lifetime which is described in seven ways:

1. ***Drink water from your own cistern* (Proverbs 5:15a)** – Here, spouses are counseled to only enjoy sex or quench their sexual thirsts from their own marriage or spouses.
2. ***…and running water from your own well* (Proverbs 5:15b)** – In the same way, the spouses are required to satisfy their strong sexual desires only in their own marriage.
3. ***Should your fountains be dispersed abroad, streams of water in the streets* (Proverbs 5:16)?** – Here, spouses are questioned to judge if it is right to break their own love-need vow to share their

exclusive sexual privileges with people outside the marriage?

4. ***Let them be only your own, and not for strangers with you*** (**Proverbs 5:17**) – Spouses are required to keep their sexual privileges exclusive to themselves in the marriage and never to be shared with people outside the marriage.

5. ***Let your fountain be blessed and rejoice with the wife of your youth*** (**Proverbs 5:18**) – The husband is admonished to keep his sexual organ blessed. In other words, he is admonished to allow his sexual organ to bring only happiness to his wife. Husbands are also encouraged to enjoy sex with the wife of their youth. This means that the spouses are required by their own love-need vows not to allow their aging process to affect the attraction, and sexual passion for each other.

6. ***As a loving deer and a graceful doe, let her breasts satisfy you at all times; and always be enraptured with her love*** (**Proverbs 5:19**) – The husband is admonished to focus his attention on the charming beauty of his wife alone. He is required to develop his sexual attraction only on the beautiful body of his wife at all times. Again, husbands are admonished to get themselves enthused, intoxicated, satisfied and content with their wife's sexual love alone. The rea-

son is that getting always enraptured or intoxicated with the beauty and sexual love of one's own wife, generates mental stronghold against the enticement from other women's beauty or seduction. To keep each other's attraction in mind is the best way to keep off the sexual charms of others from engaging the mind.

7. ***For why should you, my son, be enraptured by an immoral woman, and be embraced in the arms of a seductress* (Proverbs 5:20)?** – The husband is again, admonished to evaluate if it is right or appropriate to sexually intoxicate self with an immoral woman? This is a vice versa statement; so, the wife needs to ask herself the same question as to whether it is right to enrapture self with an immoral man?

The reasons for warning against fornication and adultery are that such immoral sexual engagements displease the Lord, it incurs His judgment, and destroys marriages. When heterosexualism, which is the attraction between man and a woman develops into relationship and then to marriage, it generates a spousal protective love of jealous. The spousal jealous love is simply the feeling of responsibility to exhibit love by protecting each other's spouse from sexual abuses.

Again, the spousal jealous love of protection is an innate responsibility each spouse feels and bears about each other. The jealous love is also about protecting the pride, loyalty, and the exclusive sexual privilege each enjoys and shares with each other. The spouses by the motivation of their love-need vows, entrust their individual life and body to each other after establishing the covenant of marriage. As a result, the spouses begin to feel the privilege and the responsibility to protect their sexual exclusive privileges they enjoy from sexual intruders.

The marital jealous love is best described in Song of Songs chapter eight and verse six which states: *Set me as a* **seal upon your heart**, *as a* **seal upon your arm**; *For love is as strong as death,* **jealousy as cruel as the grave**; *Its flames are* **flames of fire**, *a* **most vehement flame**.

First, the Shulamite or Mrs. Peace or Solomon, appealed to her husband to *set* (her) *as a seal upon* (his) *heart…* In other words, she was appealing to her husband to place her in the very part of his heart where he will not forget about his pledge of commitment to her. In vice versa, husbands, also make the same appeal directly or indirectly to their vives.

Second, she also appealed to her husband to *set* (her) … *as a seal upon* (his) *arm…* The implication here is that the wife is requesting her husband to proudly make her known in public as his significant wife to avoid any other woman to mistake him for a single man. For other men and women to mistake a significant wife or husband as single to pave way for their seduction, arouses unhealthy jealous love. Unhealthy jealous love can be as powerful and cruel as the grave and as consuming as fire. However, the genuine protective love of jealousy should not cause harm to each other because, it is a violation of the fundamental principle of love as affirmed in Scripture as follows: *Love does no harm to a neighbor; therefore, love is the fulfillment of the law* **(Romans 13:10).**

Furthermore, the violation of the husband's exclusive jealous love of protection of his wife on the other hand is also described in these strong words:

> *Whoever **commits adultery** with a **woman** (wife) lack understanding; He who does so **destroys his own soul** (incurs God's judgment). ^{33}**Wounds and dishonor** he will get, and his **reproach** will not be wiped away (human judgment). ^{34}For **jealousy is a husband's fury**; Therefore, he will not spare in the day of vengeance. ^{35}He will accept no recompense, nor will he be appeased though you give many gifts* **(Proverbs 6:32-35).**

Adultery is a serious violation in marriage because it incurs God's judgment and arouses the unhealthy jealous love of the spouses. Adultery by implication violates spousal trust and destroys the bond of marital one-fleshness. Hence, the sharing of the marital exclusive sexual privileges with others outside the marriage, defeats God's principle of marital one-fleshness and violates the spousal trust. The marital one-flesh principle is expressed in these words: *Therefore, a man shall leave his father and mother and be joined to his wife, and they shall become **one flesh*** **(Genesis 2:24).**

Adultery is indeed an attack against marital bond and it's also a fatal violation of the one-flesh principle of marriage. The one-flesh sexual bonding equation can be expressed as follows: 1 (the husband) +1 (the wife) = 1 (which is the oneness of marriage and oneness of flesh through sex). Thus, marriage with its sexual intimacy of consummation bonds the husband and his wife into one-flesh to lead to the bonding of their souls as well.

However, adultery violates and changes the one-flesh marital bonding equation to the following: 1 (the husband) +1 (the wife) +1 (sex the intruder) = 0 (marital bonding annulment). Our Lord Jesus Christ in his teachings condemned sexual immorality which refers to all manner of sexual sins against marriage. The reason is that it violates the one-flesh bond of marriage with its spousal dependability of trust **(Matthew 5:32).**

Ironically, the Twi language of Ghana translates adultery from the Bible as an act which "destroys marriage". Spouses should, therefore, encourage honest and free conversation about their sexual lives. Discovering and solving all sexual concerns together in marriage is one of the best ways to resist sexual temptations against marriage. To this end, spouses should never forget or neglect their love-need vow responsibility to keep their marriage bed pure. In other words, the husband and his wife are required by their own love-need vows of marriage to exclusively preserve their sexual organs and sexual privileges to themselves for their lifetime.

CHAPTER FIVE

VOW TO EXPRESS THE EIGHT HONORING VIRTUES TO YOUR SPOUSE FOR LIFETIME

---

*As Sarah **obeyed** Abraham, calling him **lord** (signifies honor), whose daughters you are if you do good and are **not afraid with any terror**. ⁷Husbands, likewise, dwell with them with understanding, **giving honor to the wife**, as to the **weaker vessel**, and as being heirs together of the grace of life, that your **prayers may not be hindered** (1Peter 3:6-7).*

Eight Ways For Spouses to Honor Themselves

Marriage is honorable in every culture **(Hebrews 13:4)** and the spouses by their love-need vow responsibilities are required to honor each other for a lifetime. Honor in marriage can be expressed among spouses in eight ways to prove love for each other as follows: Indispensable, respect, obedience, honesty, integrity, recognition, pampering, and giving:

(1) Spouses Are Required to Honor Themselves as Indispensable for Lifetime

Spouses by their love-need vow responsibilities are required to honor themselves as indispensable. If spouses would perceive each other as indispensable, it will motivate the esteeming of each other as absolutely necessary as scripturally affirmed: *Let nothing be done through selfish ambition or conceit, but in lowliness of mind* **let each esteem others better than himself** **(Philippians 2:3).** The honor of indispensability principle requires spouses to place high premium of absolute necessity over each other. Again, the honor of indispensability is expressed in marriage by way of treating each other like a precious gem which each spouse cannot afford to lose.

Hence, spouses by the motivation of their love are required to cherish by holding each other in high esteem and treating each other very dearly with great worth and importance. Furthermore, spouses' love-need vows are expected to motivate them to place exclusive and high value on their significant partners far above any other human as expressed between king Solomon and his wife, the Shulamite. [6] Open American Tract Society Dictionary on Power Bible CD

---
6. Staggs, Brandon. Open American Tract Society Dictionary - Shulamite. Power Bible CD, Phil Lindner, 2006.

portrays the idea that that Shulamite is the feminine name of Solomon of which both names mean peaceful. Permit me therefore, to address Solomon and his wife Shulamite as Mr. & Mrs. Peaceful.

Hence, Mrs. Peaceful, expressed her honor of indispensability of her husband, Mr. Peaceful with these words: *Like an **apple tree among the trees of the woods**, so is my **beloved among the sons**. I sat down in his shade with great delight, and his fruit was sweet to my taste* **(Song of Songs 2:3)**. Mrs. Peaceful in expressing her indispensableness of her husband, metaphorically perceived him as a blossom apple tree which bears sweet fruit amidst ordinary trees, representing all other men. She further attests that her husband is romantically enjoyable and irresistible.

In response to the indispensableness of his wife, Mr. Peaceful being motivated by his love for his wife, Mrs. Peaceful, perceived her to be invaluable, loveliest and the most favored among all other women in this romantic description: *Like a lily among thorns, So is my love among the daughters* **(Song of Songs 2:2)**. Mr. Peace further expressed the indispensability of his wife with is this beautiful metaphoric description of her: *My dove, my perfect one, is the only one, the only one of her mother, the favorite of the one who bore her. The daughters saw her and called her **blessed**, the queens and the concubines, and they praised her* **(Song of Songs 6:9)**.

King Lemuel also wrote about the honor of indispensability of a virtuous wife from the perspective of what he learned his mother. He described her as one who deserves praise: *"Many daughters have done well, but you excel them all* **(Proverbs 31:29).** Loving spouses are therefore, required to honor each other as indispensable. If spouses would perceive each other as indispensable by treating themselves as invaluable, they will not trade each other for anything in any way and of any form. In such marital honor of indispensableness, the life of marriage becomes successful and totally enjoyable.

(2) Spouses Are Required to Honor Themselves with Respect for Lifetime

Spouses by the motivation of their love-need vows are required to honor each other with respect. Spouses by the motivation of their love should honor by respecting each other's body and person. First, showing honor of respect toward each other's body is an ideal way of treating each other as endeared lovers. Spouses should be careful not to use any part of their body to create coarse jokes or to call each other demeaning names, for such expressions are proofs of each other's dishonor of disrespect toward each other's body.

Again, the use of demeaning words against each other is very dishonoring and disrespectful. Words are extremely powerful because it has the propensity to either affirm and motivate or demean and damage self-esteem as biblically cautioned: *Let your speech always be with grace, seasoned with salt, that you may know how you ought to answer each one* **(Colossians 4:6);** *Death and life are in the power of* *the tongue, and those who love it will eat its fruit* (**Proverbs 18:21**).

Second, spouses must prove their honoring by respecting each other's person. To honor by respecting each other's person goes by showing great regard for what each other thinks, feels, and wills with regards to decision inputs. Spouses must, therefore, honor themselves by respecting each other's person of intellect (mind), emotions (feelings) and volitions (will) in the following manner:

1. **Honor By Respecting Each Other's Person of Intellect** - Spouses by their own love-need vows are required to honor by respecting each other's intellectual or mental abilities. The spouses must show honor by respecting each other's knowledge, views, and suggestions. They are also supposed to honor by considering themselves as worthy of consultation and mutual planning. Disregarding each other's intellectual adequacy and planning inputs is a great disrespect of each other's person in the marriage.

2. **Honor By Respecting Each Other's Person of Emotions** - Spouses must honor by respecting each other's person of emotions by the motivation of their own love-need vows. One of the ways spouses can prove their respect to each other's emotion is to be considerate and sensitive toward each other's feelings. Arousing negative feelings of displeasure, unhealthy jealousy, distress, anger, humiliation, in-

feriority, and suppression are some of the ways of disrespecting each other's person of emotions.

3. **Honor By Respecting Each Other's Person of Volition** - Furthermore, spouses are required to honor by the motivation of their own love-need vows to respect each other's volition. The honor of respect towards each other's volition requires the spouses to mutually consult and agree on all matters of their lives and the marriage before decision. Disrespect of each other's volition could be expressed in to two ways: First, making decisions without each other's input and agreement is very disrespectful of each other's person. Second, deciding and carrying out decisions before informing your spouses is very dishonoring and disrespectful. Spouses must, therefore, do well to avoid such disrespectful attitude toward each other's person.

(3) Spouses Are Required to Honor by Obeying Themselves for Lifetime

The love-need vows of spouses require them to honor each other through obedience. Honoring each other as spouses by way of obedience is paramount to peace, happiness, and success in the marriage. Spouses are duty bound by their own love-need vows to obey by way of listening to each other's bidden, concerns and advice. Refusing to obey by listening to each other causes displeasure, confusion, and unnecessary creation of problems in the marriage.

The Bible recommends mutual submission as the core requirement of good and enjoyable marital relationship as expressed, ...*submitting to one another in the fear of God* **(Ephesians 5:21).** Sarah of old proved her understanding of honoring through obedience. She honored her husband Abraham through obedience and even accorded him the honor of lordship in the sense of high respect and unreserved submission to his bidden, concerns and advice **(1Peter 3:6).**

Since honoring and submission are reciprocal in marriage, husbands on the other hand, are required to do likewise by obeying their wives through submission and listening to their bidden, concerns and advice. The Bible requires husbands to honor their wives in the following recommendation: *Husbands, likewise, dwell with them with understanding,* ***giving honor to the wife****, as to the* ***weaker vessel****, and as being heirs together of the grace of life, that* ***your prayers may not be hindered*** (1Peter 3:7).

First and foremost, the wife's description as being the "weaker vessel" has nothing to do with her intellectual capabilities as some try to ascribe. The wife's description as the weaker vessel is in reference to her physical strength as compared to her husband. Husbands as the stronger vessels are therefore, required to protect and support their wives in any way possible.

Second, the wife's description as the weaker or less strong vessel also portrays her sensitive, deep, and delicate emotions. Wives' emotions are very sensitive, deep, and very delicate, in the sense that its complexities cannot be fully understood or predicted. Therefore, husbands are required to treat their wives with loving care. The careless arousals of a wife's negative emotions limit her efficiency as a wife in so many ways. In the same way, husbands' emotions are complex and can not be full predicted. In general, emotions are very delicate, very influential, and affective in all matters of life, requiring much wisdom to deal with it. Surprisingly, both positive and negative emotions have great impact on our health, either for good or for worse.

Emotions are naturally neutral and its negative and positive effects are resulted from either negative or positive actions, utterances, or circumstances. Hence, both spouses are required to exercise restraint on each other's actions and utterances in order to nurture healthy emotions in each other.

Three, dishonoring through disobedience by refusing to safeguard each other's emotions, does not only hinder the prayers of the husband, but it also hinders the prayers of the wife. Four, the honor of obedience in marriage has nothing to do with authority and control, but rather, it is about pleasing or displeasing each other as spouses. In fact, one of the best ways to evaluate marital honor of obedience is to ask a displeasing question and do a sincere self-answering as follows: Has my spouse been complaining about anything in our marriage concerning me? Answering this question honestly shall reveal how extensive each one has been displeasing and hurting each other through disobedience.

Apostle Paul by the love principle of reciprocity, reveals

that love must compel a person to return love of obedience and pleasure to the one who has shown love. In his case, it was about Christ who has shown great love to humanity by dying for our sins and saving our soul from damnation as affirmed in these words: *For the **love of Christ compels us**, because we judge thus: that if One died for all, then all died…* **(2 Corinthians 5:14).** By the same token, spouses by the motivation of their love must compel themselves to obey by listening and pleasing each other. The spouses should do well to develop mutual submission in order for wives to obey their husbands, and for husbands to also obey their wives by listening to each other's concerns, advice, and cautions.

Sadly, there are some husbands and wives who find it difficult to listen to each other and even apologize when they go wrong in their disobedience. There are many spouses out there who emphatically affirm to their spouses that they hate to say sorry. However, even David, the anointed king by God, proved that nobody is above submission of obeying or listening to each other stated: *So, David received from her hand what she had brought him, and said to her, "Go up in peace to your house. See, **I have heeded your voice and respected your person** (1Samuel 25:35)."* In this narrative, Nabal had mistreated David and his troop without the knowledge of his wife Abigail. After finding out, she quickly rectified the situation by providing what David and his team needed. Abigail used this opportunity to advice David against vengeance of which he respected her person by listening to her advice.

If spouses would honor each other by obedience of listening to each other's advice, concerns and cautions, life's mistakes and confusions shall be completely minimized. The love-need vow to honor each other requires mutual submission of obeying each other. One, may say, show me the spouses who do not obey by listening and respecting each other, and I will show you the spouses whose marriage is suffering and failing.

(4) Spouses Are Required to Honor Each Other With Honesty for Lifetime

The love-need vow of honoring obligates the spouses to prove their honesty to each other by way of transparency, truthfulness, and trustworthiness in words, actions, and character. In fulfilling the honor of honesty, spouses are required by their love-need vows to authenticate their marriage with the three major qualities of honesty:

1. **Honesty of Transparency** - Marital love-need vows require spouses to honor each other with the honesty of transparency. The nakedness principle which was exhibited between Adam and his wife teaches about honesty of transparency among spouses **(Genesis 2:25)**. Spouses by the motivation of transparency, should portray nakedness of openness, shamelessness, and shylessness with regards to their bodies, minds or thoughts, emotions, and incidences of their lives in the marriage. Total honesty of transpar-

ency in marriage removes suspicions and makes the spouses predictable.

2. **Honesty of Truthfulness** - Marital love-need vows require spouses to honor each other with the honesty of truthfulness. Speaking truth to each other in marriage is not an option but a requirement the spouses' own love-need vows require. The utterances and behaviors of each spouse should always correspond with the facts of reality of each other's life. When spouses dishonor each other through dishonesty, they are allowing satanic influences into their marriage as stated: *"But let your **'yes' be 'yes**,' and your **'no,' 'no.'** For whatever is more than these is **from the evil one*** **(Matthew 5:37)**. Spouse should never forget that they owe each other the truth of honesty.

3. **Honesty of Trustworthiness** - Marital love-need vows require spouses to honor each other with the honesty of trustworthiness. Trustworthiness is not an accorded quality but an earned quality in marriage. A trustworthy spouse is a spouse who had earned each other's trust and has then become worthy of the trust of faithfulness, commitment, dependability, and loyalty.

As a matter of fact, dishonesty is unconcealable, in the sense that it cannot be hidden forever. God has even pledged a promise to expose every form of dishonesty from its covering darkness with His light in these words: *"For nothing is secret that will not be revealed, nor anything hidden that will not be known and come to light* **(Luke 8:17)**. Spouses must not forget that when a hidden truth gets revealed, it will cost the dishonest spouse their trust and arouse fear of distrust in the heart of the offended spouse.

Dishonesty does not only affect the offended spouse, but rather, it burdens the dishonest spouse with great responsibility to earn back trust from the offended spouse. In fact, restoring trust in marriage may take a great deal of time and sacrifice, depending on the level of dishonesty incurred. Spouses by the motivation of their love-need vows should, therefore, commit to honor each other with honesty throughout their lifetime.

(5) Spouses Are Required to Honor Each Other Through Integrity for Lifetime

Spouses by their own love-need vows of marriage are required to honor each other with integrity. The honesty of integrity is about proving each other's consistent sound moral rightness and reliability as affirmed in these words: *He who walks with integrity walks securely, but he who perverts his ways will become known* **(Proverbs 10:9)**. Again, marital love requires the spouses to prove each other's sound moral consistency and reliability. It is always a great disappointment and betrayal for spouses to discover of each other any form of hidden immoral character or behavior. Discovery of immoral hidden behavior or character among spouses arouse the feeling of great displeasure, disappointment, and betrayal.

The first integrity principle from the referenced Scripture above teaches that if a person walks in integrity of moral rightness, security of confidence, safety and trust becomes an enjoyable reality. The second integrity principle also states *...but he who perverts his ways will become known.* The principle here is that becoming perverted or crooked in character in the course of the journey of the marriage is a choice some spouses make. However, such corrupt choices cannot be hidden forever. Hence, spouses must commit to honor each other with the virtue of integrity. Spouses must do well not to surprise each other with an unknown dishonoring character.

Moreover, developing dishonoring character in the course of the marital journey has always been detrimental to marital success and the happiness of the spouses. The feeling of disappointment in marriage arouses a great hurt, which makes a spouse feel betrayed, abused, and disrespected. I would therefore, caution spouses to live by their own love-need vows to honor each other through integrity to assure their own happiness and success of their marriage.

(6) Spouses Are Required to Honor Each Other Through Recognition for Lifetime

Spouses are required by their own love-need vows to honor each other through recognition for their lifetime. Spouses by the motivation of love are required to honor each other through recognition as a proof of their knowledge, admiration and appreciation of each other's services, attractiveness, and good deeds. Failure to honor by recognition is to indirectly and directly communicate to your spouse that you have eyes but refuse to see, ears but refuse to hear, tongue but refuse to taste, mouth but refuse to speak, nose but refuse smell and body but refuse to feel any warmth touch.

Moreover, spouses should do their possible best to consciously recognize each other by admiring, complimenting, appreciating, and affirming each other's attractiveness, services, sacrifices, giving, and other good deeds. Spouses must, therefore, accept their love-need vow responsibility to honor each other through recognition by doing the following:

1. **Honor of Recognition Through Sense of Sight** - Spouses by the motivation of their love-need vows should commit to appreciate and compliment on every delightful thing they see on each other. The expression of the honor of recognition in this manner is the way to admire and affirm each other's captivating attractiveness and self-esteem.

2. **Honor of Recognition Through Sense of Hearing** - Spouses should commit to recognize each other through their sense of hearing – Spouse must do well to find out what their spouse love to hear so that they can complement each other with it. The words of spouses should be kind and empowering

in complementing each other on admirable gestures and the kind actions they offer to each other. Recognizing each other with loving and kind words are good ways to appreciate and admire each other's beauty and good works as a motivation for more or better.

3. **Honor of Recognition Through Sense of Taste -** Spouses by their love-need vows are also required to recognize each other through their sense of taste by appreciating and complimenting on the good tastes they enjoy in the marriage. It is a way of proving to each other that they have lips and tongue to taste good food and enjoy romantic kisses from each other. To express recognition with regards to scrumptious taste from each other is by admiring and affirming each other's captivating kisses, good cooking skills and good restaurant picks.

4. **Honor of Recognition Through Sense of Smell** - Spouses must prove their honor of recognition through their senses of smell by appreciating, admiring, affirming, and complimenting on the good aroma around themselves as a proof of their sharp sense of smell. The spouse's failure to recognize each other by affirming and complimenting on the good aroma around themselves is ignoring and despising.

5. Honor of Recognition Through Sense of Touch - Marital love-need vow motivations require the spouses to express their enjoyment of each other's romantic closeness, smooches, and bodily intimacies. Appreciating, and complimenting on each other's romantic touches and mutual intimate experiences are ways to prove admiration and affirm strong desire for each other in marriage.

In summary, the honor of recognition in marriage, requires spouses to admire, appreciate, compliment, and affirm each other in all delightful and pleasing actions and gestures with regards to what each spouse say, do and offer to each other. Spouses must do well not to forget to always express their honor of recognition in admiring, appreciating, complimenting, and affirming each other's attractiveness, kind gestures, services, giving, sacrifices, and all other good deeds. In other words, spouses by the motivation of their love-need vows, should see to it that no good, delightful, and attractive deed should go unnoticed and unrecognized in their marriage.

(7) Spouses Are Required to Honor Each Other Through Gratitude for Lifetime

Moreover, spouses are required by their own love-need vows to honor each other by showing gratitude for both little and big kind gestures toward each other. The refusal to show forth gratitude of thankfulness or appreciation for each other's supports, giving and inputs is dishonoring and demoralizing. The honoring of each other through gratitude is a great motivation for each spouse to do more and offer their best beyond expectation to the marriage.

Gratitude is always proven with the return of another form of the kindness and the love enjoyed. Marginalizing gratitude in all realms of life and before God is indeed displeasing, dishonoring as was emphasized by the Lord in these words: *…and **fell down on his face at His feet, giving Him thanks.** And he was a Samaritan. ⁷So Jesus answered and said, "**Were there not ten cleansed?** But **where are the nine?** ¹⁸ Were there not any found who **returned to give glory to God** except this foreigner?* (**Luke 17:16-18**)" The negative effects of ingratitudeness, should always be a caution to spouses not to discount any kind gesture which is offered to each other as little and therefore, unworthy of gratitude. The habit of ingratitudeness among spouses is unhealthy for loving relationships because, it speaks the language of dishonor to each other as spouses.

(8) Spouses Are Required to Honor Each Other Through Pampering for Lifetime

Spouses by their own love-need vows are required to honor each other through pampering for lifetime. Pampering deals with special and excessive treatments of care and attention. Pampering in marriage is also about fulfilment of each other's gratification or yearnings through caring, special treatments, giving and serving each other.

The honoring of pampering requires the spouses' readiness and commitment to give the best of care, attention, comfort, romantic massages, smooches, gifts, and special services to each other with cheer.

In the romantic realms of pampering, there should be caring, endearment, and nourishment of each other's body through what makes the body beautiful, attractive, relaxed, and comfortable. Again, in romantic pampering, the spouses are required to give enough attention to their romantic and intimate love. When spouses pamper each other very well through cuddling and satisfying orgasmic sexual intercourse, the husband, and the wife release oxytocin into their bodies to promote their love and health. [7]According to Maureen Salamon, "oxytocin promotes attachment, solidifies relationships, eases stress, boost sexual arousal, induces sleep" and six others.

In the realms of honoring through pampering, spouses commit to satisfy each other's emotional hunger without to beg for it or give unloving excuses. To discover what makes each other emotionally hungry and thirsty, loving spouse should ask and give each other the chance to speak honestly about it. Furthermore, the spouses should be intentional to pamper each other by spending creative and quality time together. They should never allow anything to steal their precious attention from each other for their lifetime; for such is the nature of honoring through pampering of each other as husband and wife.

---

7. Salamon, Maureen. *11 Interesting Effects of Oxytocin.* 30 May 2013, https://www.livescience.com/35219-11-effects-of-oxytocin.html. Accessed 26 August, 2021.

CHAPTER SIX

VOW TO SERVE YOUR SPOUSE FOR LIFETIME

Spouses are required by their own love-need vows to serve each other cheerfully for lifetime. Marriage by its divine order calls for the responsibility of mutual serving of each other. Mutual serving in marriage makes life responsibilities bearable and its home chores less burdensome. The spouses' love-need vow to join life into oneness and commonness of purpose requires them to serve each other with all their potentials, and capabilities. Spouses are required to provide the help which is needed to reduce each other's workload or burden in any way possible as affirmed: *Bear one another's burdens, and so fulfill the law of Christ* **(Galatians 6:2).** If spouses would commit to their love-need vow to serve each other cheerfully, no one will complain about being overburdened in the home alone.

The spouses' willingness to serve each other is a prove of their embracement of the principle of the two being made into a single pool of resource for mutual benefit.

Marital home chores management through serving should not be designated only to the wife or to the husband. The uniqueness of masculinity and femininity play a role in marital serving. Any work in the marital home which requires, technicality, risks, and much vigor supposed to be done by the husband to prove his masculinity, servant leadership and family protection responsibility as affirmed in these words: *For the husband is* **head of the wife**, *as also Christ is head of the church; and* **He is the Savior of the body**. *Husbands, love your wives, just as Christ also loved the church and* **gave Himself for her,** **(Ephesians 5:23,25).**

Moreover, Christ who is God and Savior of the church even washed the feet of his close twelve disciples. If our Lord served His disciples and is still serving the church, which is His bride, why should husbands find it displeasing and difficult to serve their own loving family in any way they can? The two verses of Scripture above portrays two major serving principles as follows:

1. Just as Christ who is the head of the church has become the Savior of her, so the husband who is the servant leader of his home supposed to save his wife and children by protecting them from any harm or risks.

2. Just as Christ by the motivation of His love, gave up his life for the bride which is the church; in the same way, the husband by the motivation of his love supposed to serve, protect, and even risk life for the wife and children when the need arises. The husband

as the head or the servant leader of his home, and a potential father should not hesitate to serve his family in any way possible.

Furthermore, the husband by the motivation of his servant leadership responsibility is requirement to be an example in everything in order to serve his family in any way possible as was required of Timothy who was the pastor of the church at Ephesus: *…but be an example to the believers in **word**, in **conduct**, in **love**, in **spirit**, in **faith**, in **purity*** **(1Timothy 4:12).** Husbands as servant leaders are not supposed to only serve their family in services but they must also lead his family by example in the following virtues:

1. Husbands by the motivation of their servant leadership are required to show good and right example in word through any form of verbal expression and conversation he engages with his wife and children.

2. Husbands by the motivation of their servant leadership are required to show good and right example in conducts of behavior and attitude in every situation in the marriage.

3. Husbands by the motivation of their servant leadership are required to show good and right example in love to commit to sacrifice to meet the needs of his family and also to offer his best for his wife and children.

4. Husbands by the motivation of their servant leadership are required to show good and right example in spirit. The husband's exemplariness in the spirit of his servant leadership means that he is required to show forth right mental values and perspectives of life, right emotional attitude, and right volitional decisions in every aspect of life.

5. Husbands by the motivation of their servant leadership are required to show good and right example in faith of right relationship with God, his family, and others outside the family.

6. Husbands by the motivation of their servant leadership are required to show good and right example in purity. Purity has to deal with a mind which is free from the entertaining of evil, an emotion free from harboring of negative feelings and motivations, a volition which is free from the dictates of wrong decisions and actions and a conscience which is free guilt and condemnation.

Furthermore, the wife who is a leader alongside her husband is also required to exhibit these leadership qualities as well. Moreover, the wife is required to serve her husband and children as the home maker, the manageress, and a mother. The average wife's home making responsibilities come with a special innate capability which enables her to serve her husband, children, and home with ease.

Her typical serving responsibilities are exemplified in the lifestyle of the virtuous wife in Proverbs chapter thirty-one and verses ten through thirty-one which is treated in part two of chapter.

Serving each other as spouses requires the developing of the virtue of teachability to teach and be taught about each other's skills of services in the marital home. The romantics and the beauty about spousal serving are best seen when the spouses offer their love presence and support for each other during services in the home. Although, a particular type of service may require one person to do it. However, to offer presence during the service or work to each other is a great motivation and an encouragement. In other words, when the spouses are working together, even if it is only one person doing the work at a time, it serves as a great motivation.

Again, spouses must bear in mind that indolence of unnecessary excuses from doing what is required of each other in marriage, kills the best of what marriage has to offer to its partners. Hence, both spouses are required to be diligent and intentional in all their services so that they can please each other by their own motivation of love.

CHAPTER SEVEN

VOW TO MAKE EACH OTHER HAPPY FOR LIFETIME

Another important love-need vow spouses must admit to themselves is the responsibility to make each other happy for a lifetime. Happiness in marriage is based on what spouses intentionally and strategically commit to do, give, and say to please each other in order to arouse the feelings of excitement, respect, care, admiration, honor, contentment, and endearment. Happiness in marriage is conditionally reciprocal because spouses only enjoy it when they give it cheerfully as the royal principle of reciprocity affirms: *If you really fulfill the* **royal law** *according to the Scripture, "You shall* **love your neighbor as yourself***," you do well* (**James 2:8**) *"And just as* **you want men to do to you***, you also* **do to them likewise** (Luke 6:31).

Happiness is conditioned upon its corresponding positive actions, utterances, services, giving, and circumstances.

Therefore, spouses must remember to treat each other as emotional beings whose feelings are conditioned to either to enjoy happiness or endure sadness or distress. Emotions are neutral and they are conditioned to be aroused either positively or negatively on the basis of actions, treatments, words, expressions, and satisfaction of each other's love-needs in various ways and forms as follows:

1. Spouses must commit to use what they do, give, and say to arouse the feelings of excitement in the heart of each other.
2. The utterances, expressions, generous gestures, and actions should be geared toward making each other feel contented and appreciative by each other in the marriage.
3. If the spouses feel admired and attractive to each other, happiness becomes a natural flow in the marriage.
4. The utterances, expressions and gestures of spouses should be intended to arouse the good feeling of honor and respect as discussed in chapter five in order to arouse happiness.
5. Spouses should commit to consciously arouse the feelings of happiness by doing and saying things which make each other feel endeared, and cherished.

Furthermore, spouses must come to the realization that negative utterances, attitudes, expressions, and actions against each other has the propensity to kill the good feelings which are enjoyed by each other. If spouses' expressions and actions arouse negative feelings without care, their relationship shall become toxic and unhealthy for both spouses. Spouses should not forget that they have assumed the love-need vow responsibility to ensure each other's happiness.

The principle of reciprocity with regards to mutual happiness in marriage requires the spouses to sow happiness, in order to reap happiness. Failure to make your spouse happy is bound to stifle your own happiness in one way or the other. Spouses must again realize that their emotions are naturally and neutrally complex. For that reason, the spouses should commit to say, give, and do things the right things to arouse healthy emotions in each other. However, to err is human, so if a spouse in any way or form arouses any negative feelings, they should do well to apologize and accept each other's apology as quickly as possible.

Living with negative feelings as spouses for even a day is not healthy for both spouses. Hence, spouses should do well to resolve the causes of their negative emotions when they do get aroused. Beside the negative feelings which has the propensity to affect the relationship, it also affects the health of the spouses. The reason is that the continuous feeling of anxieties, fears, hurts, bitterness, and anger release a negative stress hormone called cortisol. Excessive and extended release of cortisol as a result of unresolved negative emotions shall affect the health of the spouses. Dr. Don Colbert (MD) in his New York bestselling book, Stress Less, asks this fact statement question which is worthy of consideration with regards to stress and its danger: [8]"Did you know that 75 to 90 percent of all visits to a primary care physician's office are related to stress disorders? That's according to the American Institute of Stress (p. 5)".

As a result, spouses must be thoughtful to commit to make all the necessary efforts to safeguard each other's emotions from being aroused negatively. Protecting each other from a continuous release of cortisol, is the greatest gift spouses can contribute to their own health. The stifling of marital happiness through unthoughtful character, behaviors and utterances creates life stress. Unrectified emotional stressors affect the mental, emotional, and physical health of the spouses. The love-need vows of spouses should, therefore, motivate them to ensure each other's happiness. The reason is that being inconsiderate toward each other's happiness does not only affect health, it also affects moods, motivations, and confidence toward each other as spouses.

---

8. Colbert, Don. Stress Less. Siloam A Strang Company, Lake Mary, 2008.

CHAPTER EIGHT

VOW TO READILY ADMIT AND FORGIVE FAULTS FOR LIFETIME

Then He said to the disciples, "It is impossible that no offenses should come, but woe to him through whom they do come
(Luke 17:1)!

The love-need vows of spouses require them to readily admit their faults and readily forgive them throughout their lifetime. The mutual submission to readily admit and forgive faults for lifetime in marriage is an emotional health and peace love-need vow in marriage. The spouses knowingly or unknowingly and consciously or unconsciously make this vow to each other at their marriage. First and foremost, spouses must come to the quick understanding and admission of the fact of life which says, "to err is human." In the introductory verse above, Jesus reminds everyone that "…*It is impossible that no offenses should come, but woe to him through whom they do come"*.

In order words, as humans as we are with our fluctuating emotions and ego of self-centeredness, selfishness, greed and pride, the offenses of displeasure in marriage are bound to be experienced among each other in the marriage. Offense in the language of conflict is usually resulted from disagreements. Disagreement in marriage results from clash of interests, selfish motivations, pride, and abuses. Moreover, the abuses in marriage are expressed in the form of taking undue advantage of each other with disrespectful utterances, demeaning criticism, and physical assaults.

Since offenses are bound to occur in marriage, the spouses must exercise their humility and mutual submission to admit faults, regret out from the faults, apologize sincerely, and change ways consciously. Intensities in offenses differ from spouses to spouses. However, loving spouses who are committed to their own vows shall see to minimize or avoid the things which cause unnecessary displeasures and disagreements.

Furthermore, the offender by the motivation of their mutual love and submission, shall see to quickly admit to faults, apologize, and do everything necessary to ensure peace as quickly as possible. In most cases, the things which cause offenses or conflicts in marriage are usually not big stuff. Most often than not, the conflict itself is always not the only problem. However, what breaks the camel's back to the extremes of conflict is usually resulted from the arrogance and self-centered attitude the offender expresses toward the offended during the conflict.

Spouses, must again, do well to understand that when it comes to emotions, there is nothing like big or small offences because any magnitude of offense can cause a certain level of displeasure in your spouse. Hence, the only way spouses can enjoy their marriage is to limit faults consciously and possibly commit to minimize or avoid them as emphasized in the following: *Repay no one evil for evil.* ***Have regard for good things in the sight of all men.***[18] *If it is possible,* ***as much as depends on you, live peaceably with all men*** **(Romans 12:17, 18).**

The enjoyment of peace and tranquility in marriage is dependent on each spouse. Meaning, spouses are the determinants of their own peace and tranquility by way of resolving conflicts quickly and trying their possible best to avoid them. Regretfully, one of the love-need vows spouses usually fail to understand and commit to uphold is resolving their conflicts. Resolving conflicts among spouses require them to minimize offences, admit faults, and forgive them quickly to avoid the harboring of grudges which generate emotional toxins.

Spouses must, therefore, develop the willingness and the commitment to resolve their conflicts by using the 24-hour window conflict settlement principle as biblically recommended: *"In your* ***anger do not sin"****: Do not let the* ***sun go down while you are still angry,*** [27] *and* ***do not give the devil a foothold*** **(Ephesian 4:26-27; NIV).** The principle here is that since anger is an element of the emotion, it can easily be aroused. However, it causes the sin problem when it is harbored, and negatively reacted upon, because the spouses refused to resolve them within the two halves of the 24 hours of the day.

Spouses must, therefore, tolerate each other's weaknesses and do well to settle all offences as quickly as possible before they retire to bed. The longer spouses sleep over offenses or conflicts, the more they toxify their relationship and intensify the damage it causes to each other and the marital relationship. The dangerous thing about unresolved offenses or conflicts is that first, it gives the devil a foothold or access into the marital relationship to cause damage. Second, unresolved conflict, have the propensity to progress to a very volatile level where it can easily consume the spouses beyond description.

The Six Damaging Progressions of Unresolved Conflicts

1. Generated Conflicts Cause Displeasures

Uncaring, unthoughtful, and inconsiderate character, behavior, attitude, and utterances arouse negative emotions which cause displeasures to each other in the marriage to create hurts.

2. Unresolved Conflict of Displeasures Progress into Hurts

Unresolved conflict of displeasures leads to emotional hurts. As emotional beings as we are, arousing negative feelings are inevitable. Therefore, spouses should expect it as part of life and must be ready to safeguard each other's emotions by minimizing conflicts and resolving them quickly. Once again, spouses must be sensitive to each other's emotions and must be conscious to minimize unnecessary tensions. Making known the emotional hurts, admitting faults, resolving them, and turning a new leaf are the ways to quench emotional fire from escalating and becoming volatile to cause damage to the marriage and each other.

3. Unresolved Hurts Progress Into Bitterness

Failure to resolve conflict at the level of displeasure and hurt shall surely progress to the level of bitterness as describe in the book of Hebrews in these words; *Pursue peace with all people, and holiness, without which no one will see the Lord:* *15looking carefully lest anyone fall short of the grace of God; lest* **any root of bitterness springing up cause trouble**, *and by this many become* **defiled** (**Hebrews 12:14,15**) as applied below:

1. In applying this passage of scripture to marital conflict, spouses are recommended to pursue peace at all costs by resolving all conflicts amicably. The reason is that unresolved conflicts erode a person's morality of doing things the right way.

2. It is very critical for the spouses to resolve their conflicts in order to enforce peace and tranquility. If spouses refuse or neglect to resolve their conflict of displeasures and hurts, they shall sprout forth the bitterness of sorrow, distress, dispiritedness,

and regrets to put the marital relationship at its disadvantage.

3. When the spouses fail to stop the growth of bitterness, it will begin to toxify or poison the good morals of the heart toward each other. According to the above Scripture, the heart of the spouses become defiled or unholy, when they allow the toxins of bitterness to permeate through the heart. In such conditions, the good contents of the heart become contaminated to cause trouble for the spouses and the marriage.

Holiness in the realms of purity of the heart can be defined as a mind which is free from the entertaining of evil thoughts and desires, an emotion free from the harboring of negative or evil feelings, and a conscience free from the uncomfortable effects of guilty with its distress. Unfortunately for everyone, the deep thoughts of the heart cannot be known by another person except God. It is only God who knows and evaluates the heart with all its contents. God, therefore, recommends to all to detoxify their hearts by resolving conflicts through forgiveness in order not to impede our relationship with Him, and with ourselves. The failure to resolve the conflicts which have resulted in in bitterness, shall escalate to resentment to cause more troubles of discomforts, and dangerous reactions in the marriage.

4. Unresolved Bitterness Progresses Into Resentment

When spouses refuse to resolve their conflict of bitterness, the emotional heat shall intensify to resentment state. Resentment is a displeasing feeling of annoyance or irritation which causes spouses to despise, ignore, reject, and seek to separate self from the offender spouse. Furthermore, when this kind of emotional tension develops, the offended spouse usually begins to withdraw his or her good services, the love of romance and intimacy from the offender. When the conflict at this level of resentment does not get resolved, it shall unfortunately spike some more intensive fire between the spouses to make the relationship more toxic and defiling to generate the trouble of anger.

5. Unresolved Resentment Progresses Into Anger

Again, if the spouses refuse to settle their differences with regards to the existing conflict of resentment, their toxic emotions shall give rise to anger. Anger is a strong feeling of displeasure that impairs the rationality of the mind, leading to unfavorable attitudes and reactions. Frist, the earlier unresolved conflicts which have so far been evolving up to resentment, shall cause a great deal of trouble in the marriage. Second, the unresolved conflict shall also impact the health of both spouses, because of the continuous release of cortisol which activates stress hormones into the body. When stress prolongs, it become a distress.

However, when unresolved conflict reaches anger level, the brain releases lots of cortisol and adrenaline. Adrenaline also releases the fight or flight empowered responses. At the anger level, the release of both cortisol, and adrenaline, alongside others, may impair the mind from rational thinking, perspective, and judgment which when not intervene early may lead to regretful reactions and actions.

The anger enabled mental impairment can be likened to being drunk or being on the highs of drugs. The reason is that anger disengages the mind from the right perceptions, judgment, and decision of life. That is why the Bible cautions against uncontrolled anger with this statement: *"In your **anger do not sin**": Do not let the **sun go down while you are still angry**,* [27]and ***do not give the devil a foothold*** **(Ephesians 4:26-27; NIV).** When the heat of anger keeps boiling without being quenched by resolving the causes of the hurts, bitterness, and resentment, anger shall give way to regrettable reactions. Reactions of anger can be categorized into three types:

Three Types of Anger

1. **Passive Anger** - When unresolved conflict of displeasure of hurt gives rise to the level of anger, some individual spouses may react to their own anger in a passive manner. By the passiveness of their anger, they will usually prove to care less of the offenses, and even refuse to respond to it. However, the passive anger reaction may seek to ignore and disregard both the offense and the offender as not worthy of time and attention which may seem to be okay.

However, it is not; because such spouses, in their reactive passive anger, usually resent and despise the offender. In doing so, the spouses in this category develop such an ignoring and despising attitude to punish the offender. They passively react in seemingly unharmful ways to arouse disrespectful, and worthlessness feelings to hurt the offender spouse to the core. If spouses refuse to settle their conflicts, it will give access to the devil to instigate the spouses against themselves to destroy the marriage.

2. **Active Anger** – The active anger is usually hasty and reactive. It usually impairs the mind from rational reflective decisions and actions which later become regretful. The Bible emphasizes the importance of controlling one's anger in these words: *He who is slow to anger is better than the mighty, and he who rules his spirit is better than he who takes a city* **(Proverbs16:32).** Spouses in this category are usually not slow to react in anger and are even not willing to control their anger from spilling out on their spouses.

Usually, such spouses in their active anger will not care to say or do anything at all to hurt their own spouse. Active anger impairs the mind and motivates angry spouses to react to their impulses which they later regret after reflecting on the damage their rush actions have caused. That is why spouses should do well not to sleep over their conflicts but should seek to settle them quickly. Spouses should give immediate attention to resolve their conflicts, because the longer it lingers in their hearts, the more trouble it shall cause to each other.

3. **Relentless Anger** - It is the type of anger that never gives up on revenge but plans and seeks the right timing to strike the offender spouse mercilessly. When spouses refuse to resolve conflict at this level, some spouses' anger may take a relentless or never forgiven turn to retaliate or punish the offender before their anger subside. The reaction of this type of anger is usually subtle and deadly.

The typical relentless anger was exhibited by Judas who was motivated by jealousy of his own master, Jesus Christ. Judas' jealousy aroused a hidden anger which led to an unreasonable criticism of his own boss, Christ Jesus, to the extent of making disrespectful comments against Him in public. The disrespectful attitude he expressed against Jesus, happened when Mary poured a very expensive oil on the feet of Jesus and wiped it with her hair. Out of jealousy, Judas commented that Mary's act of worship was a waste, because it could have been sold to care for the poor **(John 12:4-5)**. Jesus, however, revealed the mystery of her action as symbolic for the preparation of His yet to come burial.

Furthermore, Judas's unreasonable relentless jealous anger against Jesus motivated him to sell him out to his enemies for thirty pieces of silver as affirmed in these words: *So,* ***from that time he sought opportunity to betray Him*** **(Matthew 26:16).** Just as the relentless anger seeks to exact punishment in a subtle way, Judas at the very deep darkness of the night broke into the prayer grounds of Jesus and got Him arrested by soldiers. Spouses must, therefore, make every effort to deescalate their conflicts by resolving them quickly and amicably so that they shall not reach its dangerous apex of hate.

6. Unresolved Anger Progresses Into Hate

Finally, when spouses refuse to resolve their conflicts at the anger level, it will surely escalate to a climax of hate which the Bible terms as murder as stated thus: *Whoever* ***hates his brother is a murderer****, and you know that* ***no murderer has eternal life abiding in him*** **(1John 3:15).** One may ask, what exactly is hate? Hate is an intense dislike which always imagines evil and seeks to exact deadly punishments on the hatred, which is motivated from negative nurtured emotions. Hate also impairs judgment and motivates evil desires and deadly reactions against the hatred despite its consequences.

As mentioned earlier, when unresolved conflict reaches the apex of hate, it begins to release high cortisol of stress hormones which lead to restlessness until something brutal is done to the hatred. Moreover, when anger reaches hate level, it also releases a high level of adrenaline which gives an extraordinary strength to fight or flee depending on what is planned to be done. Hate is a very dangerous emotion because it motivates the hater to desire and seek the fatal downfall of the hatred. The hater does not relent but finds ways and means to orchestrate a punishment of destruction or death against the hatred.

At the anger and hate level, satanic influence becomes extraordinarily strong to motivate a person to fulfill the three main damaging agenda of Satan. The Bible affirms that Satan who is the ultimate thief and influencer of evil only comes with the three major aims to steal, kill, and destroy **(John 10:10).** First, anger cum hate have the propensity to motivate the hater to find every way and means to steal the honor, the beauty, and the best of life from their partners as a form of punishment. Second, there are others who will take it to the extreme by killing their own spouses to prove their point, of which they immediately regret after facing its criminal consequences. One may wonder the number of people who are in various prisons throughout the world as a result of hateful crimes.

Third, there are many other spouses who destroy each other with extreme verbal and physical abuses. They usually intend for their abuses to cause pain, suffering and harm to each other's self-esteem. When anger gives rise to hate, people imagine evil and react wickedly as was portrayed by Cain against his brother in these words: … *Sin is crouching at the door, eager to control you. But you must subdue it and be its master* **(Genesis 4:7).** When God cautioned Cain to rule over his unreasonable anger of hate, he refused, and it later motivated him to kill his own brother for no reason at all **(Genesis 4:8-9)**.

I, therefore, would like to remind all spouses of their love-need vow responsibility to settle all their differences, disagreements, and conflicts quickly and amicably. The love-need vow to resolve conflicts in marriage, first, requires the spouses to speak openly about their displeasures. Second, the spouses must admit their faults inarguably. Third, they must quickly forgive, and fourth, rectify all their faults intentionally in order to deescalate their negative emotional thoughts and reactions. The Bible recommends to all people and all spouses to have a great restraint over their negative emotions, reactions, and decisions as stated: *Repay no one evil for evil. Have regard for good things in the sight of all men.*[18]*If it is possible, as much as depends on you, live peaceably with all men.*[19]*Beloved, do not avenge yourselves, but rather give place to wrath; for it is written, "Vengeance is Mine, I will repay," says the Lord.* [20] *Therefore "If your enemy is hungry, feed him; If he is thirsty, give him a drink; For in so doing, you will heap coals of fire on his head."* [21]**Do not be overcome by evil, but overcome evil with good** **(Romans 12:17-21)**.

Spouses must, therefore, remind themselves of their own love-need vow responsibility to readily admit faults, forgive faults and rectify faults quickly. Failure to let go of ego from a loving relationship is to cause the unresolved conflicts to give rise to displeasures, hurts, bitterness, resentment, anger and to hate. I, therefore, recommend to all spouses to adopt the biblically recommended 24-hour conflict resolution principle for all offenses or conflicts that may arise in marriage. If the spouses would commit to apply the 24-hour conflict resolution principle, they can ensure their own emotional health and peace within their marriage. The healthier the emotions of the spouses, the better, and happier their marital relationship becomes.

CHAPTER NINE

VOW TO HAVE ALL THINGS IN COMMON FOR LIFETIME

The agreement to marry requires each person their love-need vow commitment to have all things in common for lifetime. The love-need vow responsibility to have all things in common in marriage, requires the spouses to agree on undertaking a particular three ventures together: First, the spouses must live together for mutual support and satisfaction. Second, spouses are required to work together toward common goals of life. Third, the spouses are required to put their resources together, invest the resources and enjoy its ownership and benefits mutually:

1. Spouses Must Live Together for Mutual Support and Satisfaction

The love-need vows of marriage require the spouses to live together for mutual support and satisfaction. The union of marriage as was intended by God is to provide mutual support and satisfaction to each other's needs as husband and wife. Ecclesiastes chapter four and verses nine through twelve teach about six benefit principles of togetherness which clearly fits into marital relationship as follows: (a) *Two are better than one, because they have a good reward for their labor.* [10] *(b) For if they fall, one will lift up his companion. (c) But woe to him who is alone when he falls, for he has no one to help him up.* [11] *(d) Again, if two lie down together, they will keep warm; But how can one be warm alone?* [12] *(e) Though one may be overpowered by another, two can withstand him. (f) And a threefold cord is not quickly broken:*

1. *Two are better than one, because they have a good reward for their labor* **(Ecclesiastes 4:9)** – The principle here is that if the two unique heterosexual persons unite in marriage to pursue a common future for themselves, they can expect a great yield for their mutual investments. The combination of the spouses' efforts and resources of time, knowledge, wisdom, expertise, strength, and finances for common marital investments and purposes, are sure to yield greater results and benefits for their enjoyment.

2. *For if they fall, one will lift up his companion* **(Ecclesiastes 4:10a)** – The love-need vows require the spouses to live together to provide mutual reliable support base for each other in their marital journey. The good thing about marital union is that if one of the spouses experience any physical, or psychological problem of any kind, support is readily

available to see each other through to the expected recovery. Mutual support can be depended upon in marriage because it is best and beautifully expressed in marriage as recommended: *Bear one another's burdens, and so fulfill the law of Christ* (**Galatians 6:2**). Again, spouses are required by their own love-need vow responsibility to assure themselves to bear each other's burdens of life together without regret or future disappointments.

3. *But woe to him who is alone when he falls, for he has no one to help him up* (**Ecclesiastes 4:10b**) – Spouses are required by their own love-need vows to alleviate marital aloneness which has the propensity to lead to loneliness. The benefit portrayed in this statement is that marriage by God's purpose should serve as the remedy for aloneness which usually leads to loneliness. One of the disadvantages of aloneness is that it deprives a person of physical backup help or support. Loneliness on the other hand deprives a person of both mental and emotional backup support as stated: *But woe to him who is alone when he falls, for he has no one to help him up…*Spouses' must, therefore, serve as each other's physical, mental and emotions support system and backup throughout their lifetime.

4. *Again, if two lie down together, they will keep warm; But how can one be warm alone* (**Ecclesiastes 4:11**)? – Spouses by their own love-need vows are required to express deep and warming romantic love to each

other. One of the benefits of marriage is that it makes the love of romance readily available and enjoyable to each other. The love touches, smooches, closeness, and intimacy in marriage are what keep the spouses physically and emotionally warm, due its good and inexpressible feelings. Spouses are therefore, cautioned not to create together-but-alone atmosphere in their marriage, because it shall lead to loneliness to affect their own happiness.

5. *Though one may be overpowered by another, two can withstand him* (**Ecclesiastes.4:12a**) – The love-need vows of spouses require them to serve as each other's reinforced protective strength. In this principle, the unique strengths of each spouse supposed to reinforce each other's weaknesses. When the spouses' strengths compensate for each other's weaknesses, they have made themselves prone-free from any physical and psychological attacks. The combined strength and the joint efforts of the spouses empower them to triumph over every situation or circumstances that may come their way for a lifetime.

6. *And a threefold cord is not quickly broken* (**Ecclesiastes 4:12b**) – The love-need vows of spouses require them to firmly unite and cleave in every way possible in order to make their marital relationship inseparably secured. The metaphorical threefold cord or strand with regards to marriage is the combined or cleaving forces of the marriage. The three uniting powerful forces of marriage include the husband and his wife

with God as their foundation, witness, ultimate help, and the reminder of spouses' vow to meet each other's needs for lifetime.

Hence, for God to be able to ensure the inseparableness or the unbrokenness of the marriage, the spouses must commit to make each other happy. The spouses are able to make each other happy by meeting each other's love needs selflessly for their lifetime. Interestingly enough, marital success and happiness is neither based on destiny nor luck. Rather, it is a choice both the husband and his wife must make to ensure and secure their own happiness and success of their marriage.

To ensure marital success and happiness, the spouses must develop the willingness and commitment to follow the principles which are enshrined in this book. By doing so consciously to fulfill each other's love-need vows to each other, happiness and marital success shall not only be a dream, but it shall be an enjoyable reality. The Bible again affirms that … *The man who finds a wife finds a treasure, and he receives favor from the LORD* **(Proverbs 18:22; NLT)**.

The implication of this verse portrays a three vice versa principle in marriage. First, if a man finds a woman he loves, marries her, and commit to love her sincerely, the wife shall become an enriching treasure of resources to him and the success of the marriage. Second, if the woman also accepts his love proposal and marries him and correspondingly commit to love him sincerely, the husband shall become an enriching treasure of resources to her and the success of the marriage.

Third, if couples shall contract marriage with such an understanding and commitment, they shall be favored by God. Favored by God means, the spouses have won God's delight and good pleasure which attracts His unlimited blessings. God's unlimited blessings fulfills the required conditions of life which bring an overflow of happiness in the lives of people, and in this this case, the spouses, and the marriage.

2. Spouses Are Required to Work Together Toward Common Goals

The love-need vows of spouses require them to have all things in common by working together toward common goals. Spouses should not acknowledge their union as partnership only, but also as a team of unique persons with unique capabilities and qualities. Working together as a team in marriage is an obligation based on the spouses' love-need vows of marriage. Additionally, relating to each other in marriage as a team toward a common goal for mutual benefit inspires dependability and future security. Enforcing team spirit in marital partnership empowers both the husband and the wife to achieve greater success together for mutual benefit.

3. Spouses Are Required to Utilize and Mutually Enjoy Ownership of their Resources.

Spouses by their love-need vows are required to utilize and mutually enjoy the ownership of their resources for lifetime. The heterosexual principle of marriage provides the relationship with special and unique resources of time, strength, potentials, knowledge, wisdom, expertise, and finances. To have all things in common in marriage requires the spouses to utilize their combined resources to achieve greater goals of their lives and to enjoy the fruit of their labor mutually. The spouses must, therefore, fulfill their love-need vow to combine all their resources for achieving the best in their lives.

Each spouse can do what they do best within their potentials and expertise with the agreement and support from each other. However, whatever business each one engages in, it must be mutually owned and benefitted to assure each other of a common future security. The early church practiced the all-in-common principle as stated: *Now all who believed were together, and* **had all things in common***, 45 and sold their possessions and goods, and divided them among all, as anyone had need* **(Acts 2:44-45).**

If the principle of having all things in common was applicable to a greater number of people, why can it be applicable to the family unit called marriage, of which its mode of operation is based on love, agreement, and oneness. The all-in-common principle as portrayed in the early church is reiterated as follows: *(1) Now the multitude of those who believed were of* **one heart and one soul***; (2)* **neither** *did anyone say that any of the things he possessed* **was his own***, but* **they had all things in common (Acts 4:32)***; (3)* **Nor was there anyone** *among them* **who lacked***; (4) for all who were* **possessors of lands or houses sold them, and brought the proceeds of the things that were sold** (Acts 4:34)…

In applying this passage of Scripture above to marriage, spouses by the motivation of their love-need vows are therefore, required to assume four basic principles to their marriage. These four basic principles must motivate spouses to have all things in common in order to meet their love-needs and pave way for success in their marriage as follows:

1. *Now the multitude of those who believed were of one heart and one soul* (**Acts 4:32a**) – The love-need vows of spouses require them to be of one heart and one soul. The couples who have trusted themselves into marriage are first required to unify their hearts of intuition and conscience. To unify the heart of intuition is for the spouses to make available to the marriage their innovative ideas, knowledge and understanding in order to ensure the success of the marriage.

    Moreover, unifying the heart of conscience requires the spouses to commit to their moral values of right and wrongs in order not to arouse unnecessary hurts and displeasures in each other. In other words, spouses must be conscious to refrain from doing the wrong things against each other; and must also be conscious to exhibit what is right toward each other. Second, spouses must unify their soul by respecting and tapping into each other's intellect of mind, emotions of feelings and volitions of mutual decision abilities to ensure the best for their lives.

2. *...neither did anyone say that any of the things he possessed was his own, but they had all things in common* (**Acts 4:32b**) – Spouses by the motivation of their love-need vows are not supposed to claim ownership to anything in their lives and the

marriage. First, marriage requires the spouses to hand over the authority of their bodies to each other after the marriage. To even refuse to turn over each other's bodily authority to each other is considered marital defrauding **(1 Corinthians 7:4-5).** Second, the spouses are required to mutually own all their resources in the marriage. To marry and still do self-claims of resources in the marriage as one's own is a violation of marital oneness or all-in-common principle of marriage.

3. *Nor was there anyone among them who lacked* **(Acts 4:34a)** – The love-need vows of marriage require the spouses to combine resources to care for the needs of each other, the marital expenses, and the prosperity of their future. The all-in-common principle in marriage, requires the spouses to make all resources available to meet each other's needs so that no one will lack any good thing in the marriage.

4. *... for all who were possessors of lands or houses sold them, and brought the proceeds of the things that were sold* **(Acts 4:34b)**... - The love-need vows further require the spouses to apply the all-in-common principle to their marriage. The spouses are to apply this principle by committing to bring together all their inner and external resources to empower themselves to achieve the best of life and attain their goals quicker for mutual benefit.

To this end, the challenge is placed before all serious-minded spouses who truly desire to enjoy marriage with all its benefits to commit to fulfill their love-need vow of having all things in common in their marriage. However, one of the major areas of marital life which requires the application of all-in-common principle is finances in marriage.

The upcoming last chapter is dedicated to the exploration of the eight types of marital financial plans. Out of the eight financial plans, it is only two which are recommendable for spouses who are motivated by love to pursue the marital journey for mutual happiness, success and benefit. The financial plan the spouses may choose shall determine the kind of marriage they can enjoy.

Finances play a major role in marriage; it can make and unmake the successes of marriages. It can also determine the kind of success, peace, happiness, and security the spouses can mutually enjoy. Frankly and practically, the eight financial plans I have put together are not new. They are marital plans spouses around the world have been and are using to manage their marital finances and are enjoying its good benefits or displeasures.

CHAPTER TEN

VOW TO CHOOSE THE RIGHT MARITAL FINANCIAL PLAN FOR LIFETIME

The love-need vows of spouses require them to choose the right marital financial plan for lifetime by committing to apply the all-in-common financial principles for their marriage. Marital financial plans with its management have been one of the things which have been posing a great deal of challenge for many spouses all around the world. In fact, all spouses who desire to enjoy peace, tranquility, and prosperity in their marriage must commit to choose a workable financial plan which will bring them together than to set them apart.

So far, I have explored and itemized at least eight types of marital financial plans spouses have adopted to manage their own marital life and home. However, some of them are inconsistent with biblical purpose of marriage and have therefore, resulted in various forms of disagreements and confusions in so many marriages. From an ideal perspective, I will recommend the first two plans out of the eight to which spouses can assure themselves of oneness, success, and happiness. The last plan, which is the eighth one however, is circumstantial plan which is usually initiated by unforeseen or solution-oriented situations:

(1) Mutual or All-In-Common Financial Plan

The mutual or the all-in-common financial plan is the number one ideal way to manage and utilize marital finances. In the mutual or all-in-common financial plan, the spouses are required by their own love-need vows to consolidate all their income into one common or family account. The spouses must then use their joint income to furnish their personal and home expenses. Marital financial plan must be guided and managed by rules, and the following are the rules for the all-in-one financial plan:

1. There should be no circumstances by which a spouse may claim ownership of some part or the entire financial resources. Under this financial plan, all what belongs to him, also belongs to her, and all what belongs her also belongs to him, no matter the amount from each other's income. All-in-common financial plan, rather, requires genuine partners who have married by the motivation of love, to classify each other's income as family or spousal mutual resource.

2. Each spouse supposed to have a copy of the debit card and to have a direct access to the mutual bank account for checks and balances.

3. Spouses must allocate a budget to pay all bills and expenses of their lives and home from the mutual or family account.

4. A personal spending limit without asking for permission must be set and agreed upon by the spouses. However, when there must be a spending beyond the agreed spending limit, it should be discussed and agreed upon before spending.

5. Each spouse must have the right to use some of the money within budget to buy a gift for each other without any consultation.

6. Benevolent giving apart from regular tithe and weekly church offering should be discussed and agreed upon before disbursing.

7. Finally, besides the budgeted spending, spouses must allocate the rest of their money into savings, investments, and any desired agreed projects. The mutual or all-in-common financial plan is the ideal plan for spouses to build a secured and mutually owned future for themselves.

(2) Petty Cash Mutual Financial Plan

The petty cash mutual financial plan is very much like the first plan whereby, each spouse brings all their income into the mutual family account to take care of all the family and personal expenses. The only difference is that instead of making all personal expenses from the family account under specific set limit, an equal petty cash amount is designated into each other's personal account to be used for personal unbudgeted expenses.

The amount allocation must be decided based on how much is left after the monthly general budget for expenses and savings. Based on the monthly surplus, a specific equal amount is then allocated to each other's personal account for personal use without seeking any permission form each other. Any personal spending which cannot be funded from each other's personal account, should be discussed, and be agreed upon before spending from the family account. The same guiding rules for the first plan also apply to this plan. This kind of financial plan also assures spouses of a secured future being built for mutual benefit and enjoyment.

(3) Equal Percent Income Financial Plan

In the equal percent income financial plan, the spouses agree to bring an equal percentage amount from each other's income into the mutual or family account to only fend for the family monthly budget. For example, the spouses may agree to bring an equal 60% from each other's income into the family account to take care of their monthly budget. However, personal expenses are not included in the monthly budget. The agreed equal percent from each spouse's weekly or bi-weekly income goes into the family mutual account to meet the family budgeted bills and other home upkeeps. Each spouse's remainder percent amount is then deposited into each other's personal account to be spent and managed without restriction or consultation. There are several problems with this kind of financial plans as follows:

1. Each spouse gets the opportunity to keep an amount depending on how low or high their income is. This means that the higher or lower your income, the higher or lower each spouse get to keep to themselves, respectively. This financial plan creates imbalance in the marriage, it arouses jealousy and discourages marital oneness or togetherness.

2. It creates the separation mentality that the spouses are not in the marriage to build a common future for mutual benefit.

3. The spouses cannot have a greater result for their labor because they have limited the mutual family finances which are supposed to enable the spouses to invest into a future, they can call their own and enjoy mutually.

4. Again, the equal percent income financial plan removes the marital focus from loving and building together for mutual benefit to a competition. The reason is that each spouse will be motivated to channel their energy and resources to building their income for their personal future. In fact, this kind of financial plan will subsequently create marital

relationship toxins which will not augur well for the success and happiness of the marriage. The financial marital competition will then generate into irresolvable conflicts in the course of time to put the relationship in jeopardy.

(4) High-to-Low Percent Financial Plan

In the high-to-low percent financial plan, the husband as the lead assumes a higher contributing income percentage to be brought into the family or the mutual account. The wife is then asked to assume a lesser percent of the family budget. This kind of financial plan is calculated based on the total monthly family budget. In this kind of financial plan, the husband on the basis of the total budget of the month may choose to contribute 60% or 70% or even more depending on his income. In the high to low percent financial plan, the husband usually decides on how much high percentage he wants to contribute to furnish the monthly budget. In fact, this plan may sound very noble, but it shall pose several problems to marriage in the course of time as follows:

1. The high to low percentage financial plan defeats the oneness, togetherness, and the commonness purpose of marriage.

2. It suggests to the wife that her husband is not in the marriage to build a common future with her. Rather her husband is just showing favor to a woman who needs desperate financial help to survive.

3. It depicts the husband as a sufficient person who does not really need a wife to make it in life.

4. It also restricts or limits the wife's right in the life of the husband and the decisions of the marital home. This is because he contributes the higher percent of the monthly budget.

However, there are some dysfunctional or survival marital relationships which may function with this type of plan. The reason is that the spouses do not trust each other financially and they are not willing to put resources together to build a common future. They only want to live together, enjoy each other's company, take care of their children and home expenses. Truthfully, this is not how God intended a successful and a happy marriage to be. As a result, this type of marriage, operating with this type of financial plan shall know no true happiness and prosperity.

(5) High-to-Low Income Authority Financial Plan

In a high-to-low income authority financial plan, the spouses bring all their income into the mutual or family account. However, the higher income earner spouse becomes the final authority in the marriage. The higher income earner spouse gets to decide on how their family financial resources should be disbursed after meeting their monthly budget. The challenges in this kind of financial plan are as follows:

The higher income earner spouse usually becomes tempted to treat the lower income earner as a non-equal person because the higher income earner has become the final authority in everything in the marriage. Thus, the master and servant kind of relationship.

1. The lower income earner begins to feel inferior to the higher income earner spouse.

2. The lower income earner begins to feel disassociated from the good future of the marriage.

3. If the wife becomes the higher income earner and the final authority, then God's plan of servant-leadership and accountability in the marital home has been compromised.

4. On the other hand, if the husband, becomes the higher income earner, and gets to decide on behalf of the family alone, he has also violated the all-in-common and partnership principle of marriage and has therefore, become a wife bully.

(6) Roommate or 50/50 Financial Plan

The roommate or the 50/50 financial plan is a kind of plan whereby the spouses decide to share all the bills and the home expenses equally or partially equal. The spouses in this plan, usually budget for all the expenses of the month and share it in two equal parts or 50/50. In some situations, the husband may decide to bring in money to cover for the mortgage or the rent with some few other things and the wife will provide to cover for all the bills, food, laundry and children's day care and other unbudgeted expenses. The challenges in this kind of financial plan are as follows:

1. The roommate or the 50/50 financial plan defeats the marital purpose of working together to build a better and a prosperous future to be mutually enjoyed. This is because each spouse refuses to combine resources for greater achievements for mutual benefit.

2. Just as the name goes, the roommate financial plan, is indeed a kind of roommate relationship which does not have a common future.

3. This plan shall gradually lead to the sharing of the home chores equally.

4. The roommate financial plan actually gives each spouse the right to keep the authority over their own bodies and lives. This shall lead to the relinquishing of each other's right over each individual's life, even to the irregulation of marital sexual life.

5. The roommate financial plan shall finally render marriage to the relationship of convenience. In the sense that it shall allow each spouse to do whatever pleases self and self alone. It shall also limit sexual enjoyment to whenever it is mutually convenient for each other. The roommate financial plan also defeats

God's purpose of oneness or all-in commonness of marriage.

(7) The Uninterrupted Sole Provider Financial Plan

In the uninterrupted sole provider financial plan, the dynamic is that the husband decides to become the uninterrupted sole provider for every expense of their home, thereby, encouraging the wife to keep her income for her personal needs without the husband's permission. Firstly, this financial plan gives the wife the leeway to spend her own money as she wishes. Secondly, the husband also gets the leeway to keep all his financial resources in his personal account for his own use without the wife's permission. The uninterrupted sole provider financial plan free the sole provider from becoming accountable to his wife and wields to him great freedom to do things his way without the wife's input. Moreover, this plan gives both spouses the right to keep the privacy of their finances without questions from each other. The challenges of this financial plan are as follows:

1. The uninterrupted sole provider financial plan creates the propensity for the husband to wield higher authority. This can easily render the wife's influence in the marriage very minimal and inputs very insignificant to the plans and decisions of the husband for their marital home.

2. It makes oneness, togetherness, and commonness in marriage impossible.

3. The marital future security becomes compromised because each spouse becomes limited in knowledge to the future prospects and endeavors of each other.

4. It creates an unforeseen chasm which will trap the marriage into its gulf in the course of time.

5. The uninterrupted sole provider financial plan removes the interdependent reliance which marriage establishes to lead to its success, happiness, and security. In order words, both spouses cannot depend on each other for their future security.

(8) Sole Provider Financial Plan

The sole provider financial plan is the plan whereby one person becomes the bread-winner due to circumstances beyond the spouses' control. If situation like this arises, it should not change any of the principles of the all-in commonness of marital relationship. This type of situation is usually temporary, and it should not give the breadwinner the audacity to be the deciding spouse in the marriage. By the motivation of love, the spouses get to mutually enjoy everything without any ill-feelings.

The caution then is this, the income handicapped spouse should never be caused to feel dependent and at the mercy of the breadwinner; because two is better than one for when one falls the other spouse by the motivation of love should help the financially fallen spouse up **(paraphrased -Ecclesiastes 4:9-10).** However, the encouragement is that the income handicapped spouse should put in every effort to find a job. Unless of course, the breadwinner does not want the other spouse to work due to other areas of their lives requiring uninterrupted attention from work.

However, it always works best to have a housewife than to have a househusband when the circumstances call for it. If the husband becomes the househusband, he should be motivated by love as a servant leader to attend to the chores in the home whiles the wife goes to work. He should also be motivated by love to attend to his wife when she returns from work. The loving husband should do well to take care of the business of the house whiles the wife is out there to bring in money to care for their lives and home.

It shall be very disappointing to every wife if the househusband stays home but refuse to care for the home to show love and appreciation to the wife when she arrives from work. In vice versa case, if the wife becomes the housewife, she also has to be motivated by love to care for the needs of the home and her husband when he arrives from work. The wife should not desist from doing what she does best for her family just for the fact of becoming the breadwinner.

Finally, if the situation requires either of the spouses to stay home and attend to the needs of the home, nothing should change with regards to fulfilling each other's love-need vow responsibilities to each other. The affection the wife needs should not be denied, and the love of respect the husband needs should not be denied. As a matter of fact, no unexpected life situation should change the dynamics of the marital love-need vow responsibilities to each other.

The marital love rule of thumb is that when one falls, supportive help should be readily available from each other in the marriage.

Please, you may contact the team of Dr. Samuel Mainoo to schedule him for speaking engagements on marriage, leadership and on any ministry topic by the following contacts:

- raphacounselingsolutions@gmail.com
- sm@raphacounselingsolutions.com
- www.raphacounselingsolutions.com

Follow Dr. Samuel Mainoo on the following social media platforms:

Rapha Counseling Solutions or Samuel Mainoo